Century 21 SOUTH-WESTERN Accounting 9E

Multicolumn Journal
Recycling Problems
Working Papers
Teacher's Edition

Claudia Bienias Gilbertson, CPA
Teaching Professor
North Hennepin Community College
Brooklyn Park, Minnesota

Mark W. Lehman, CPA
Associate Professor
School of Accountancy
Mississippi State University
Starkville, Mississippi

Australia · Brazil · Canada · Mexico · Singapore · Spain · United Kingdom · United States

SOUTH-WESTERN
CENGAGE Learning

Recycling Problems Working Papers, Teacher's Edition, Multicolumn Journal, Century 21 Accounting, 9E

**Claudia Bienias Gilbertson, CPA;
Mark W. Lehman, CPA**

VP/Editorial Director: Jack W. Calhoun

VP/Editor-in-Chief: Karen Schmohe

VP/Director of Marketing: Bill Hendee

Sr. Marketing Manager: Courtney Schulz

Marketing Coordinator: Gretchen Wildauer

Marketing Communications Manager: Terron Sanders

Production Manager: Patricia Matthews Boies

Content Project Managers: Diane Bowdler, Jenny
   Ziegler

Consulting Editor: Bill Lee

Manufacturing Buyer: Kevin Kluck

Production Service: LEAP Publishing Services, Inc.

Compositor: GGS Book Services, Inc.

Cover Designer: Nick & Diane Gliebe, Design Matters

Cover Images: Getty Images, Inc.

For product information and technology assistance, contact us at
Cengage Learning Academic Resource Center, 1-800-423-0563

For permission to use material from this text or product,
submit all requests online at **www.cengage.com/permissions**
Further permissions questions can be emailed to
permissionrequest@cengage.com

ISBN-13: 978-0-538-44714-0
ISBN-10: 0-538-44714-1

South-Western Cengage Learning
5191 Natorp Boulevard
Mason, OH 45040
USA

Cengage Learning products are represented in Canada by
Nelson Education, Ltd.

For your course and learning solutions, visit **school.cengage.com**

Printed in the United States of America
1 2 3 4 5 6 7 12 11 10 09 08

THE TEACHER'S EDITION

The Teacher's Edition of the *Recycling Problems Working Papers* for Chapters 1–24 of CENTURY 21 ACCOUNTING, 9E contains the same forms as the Student's Edition, but all the solutions are overprinted in bold italic type.

Working papers are provided for the Recycling Problems. Narrative for the Recycling Problems appear in Appendix D of CENTURY 21 ACCOUNTING. The solutions appear in this Teacher's Edition in the same sequence as the problems are presented in the Student's Edition.

PREPARING TRANSPARENCIES WITH THE TEACHER'S EDITION

Any page of this Teacher's Edition may be used as a master for making a transparency for use with the over-head projector. For best results, follow the instructions of the manufacturer of the transparency materials and the copying equipment being used in your school. Occasionally, because of the age of the materials or the equipment, some experimentation in making transparencies may be necessary.

This Teacher's Edition has been 3-hole-punched so that it may be placed in the Teacher's Resource Binder.

Contents

1-1 RECYCLING PROBLEM, p. D-1

Determining how transactions change an accounting equation

1., 2.

Trans. No.	Assets				= Liabilities	+ Owner's Equity
	Cash	+ Accts. Rec.—Dean Mills	+ Supplies	+ Prepaid Insurance	= Accts. Pay.—Topline	+ Brian Frizza, Capital
Beg. Bal. 1.	2,200 −120	− 0 −	1,100	200	200	3,300 −120 (expense)
New Bal. 2.	2,080 +400	− 0 −	1,100	200	200	3,180 +400 (investment)
New Bal. 3.	2,480 −600	− 0 −	1,100	200	200	3,580 −600 (expense)
New Bal. 4.	1,880 +425	− 0 −	1,100	200	200	2,980 +425 (revenue)
New Bal. 5.	2,305	− 0 −	1,100 +310	200	200 +310	3,405
New Bal. 6.	2,305	− 0 − +500	1,410	200	510	3,405 +500 (revenue)
New Bal. 7.	2,305 −250	500	1,410 +250	200	510	3,905
New Bal. 8.	2,055 −700	500	1,660	200	510	3,905 −700 (expense)
New Bal. 9.	1,355 +400	500 −400	1,660	200	510	3,205
New Bal. 10.	1,755 −200	100	1,660	200	510 −200	3,205
New Bal. 11.	1,555 −225	100	1,660	200 +225	310	3,205
New Bal. 12.	1,330 +675	100	1,660	425	310	3,205 +675 (revenue)
New Bal. 13.	2,005 −1,000	100	1,660	425	310	3,880 −1,000 (withdrawal)
New Bal. 14.	1,005	100	1,660	425	310	2,880
New Bal. 15.						
New Bal.						

2-1   RECYCLING PROBLEM, p. D-2

Analyzing transactions into debit and credit parts

1., 2.

Cash			
(1)	4,500.00	(2)	520.00
(4)	400.00	(4)	300.00
(11)	2,300.00	(5)	200.00
(11)	800.00	(10)	120.00
(13)	250.00	(15)	40.00
(30)	300.00	(16)	350.00
		(22)	70.00
		(23)	160.00
		(26)	1,200.00

Accts. Rec.—Flowerama			
(8)	450.00	(13)	250.00

Accts. Rec.—Seaside Inn			
(25)	640.00	(30)	300.00

Supplies			
(4)	300.00		
(9)	700.00		
(12)	300.00		

Prepaid Insurance			
(5)	200.00		

Accts. Pay.—Pacific Paper			
		(12)	300.00

Accts. Pay.—Raffi Supplies			
(16)	350.00	(9)	700.00

Luke Harris, Capital			
		(1)	4,500.00
		(11)	2,300.00

Luke Harris, Drawing			
(26)	1,200.00		

Sales			
		(4)	400.00
		(8)	450.00
		(11)	800.00
		(25)	640.00

Advertising Expense			
(23)	160.00		

Miscellaneous Expense			
(15)	40.00		

Rent Expense			
(2)	520.00		
(10)	120.00		

Repair Expense			

Utilities Expense			
(22)	70.00		

3-1 RECYCLING PROBLEM, pp. D-2, D-3

Journalizing transactions and proving and ruling a journal

JOURNAL — PAGE 1

	DATE		ACCOUNT TITLE	DOC. NO.	POST. REF.	GENERAL DEBIT	GENERAL CREDIT	SALES CREDIT	CASH DEBIT	CASH CREDIT	
1	20-- Aug.	1	Adeline Stein, Capital	R1			8 7 5 0 00		8 7 5 0 00		1
2		2	Supplies	C1		5 0 0 00				5 0 0 00	2
3		3	Rent Expense	C2		3 0 0 00				3 0 0 00	3
4		4	Supplies	M1		1 2 0 0 00					4
5			Accts. Pay.—Rim Supply				1 2 0 0 00				5
6		5	Utilities Expense	C3		2 5 0 00				2 5 0 00	6
7		8	Accts. Pay.—Rim Supply	C4		7 0 0 00				7 0 0 00	7
8		8	✔	T8	✔			4 2 5 00	4 2 5 00		8
9		8	Accts. Rec.—M. Bien	S1		1 2 5 00		1 2 5 00			9
10		9	Prepaid Insurance	C5		1 9 0 0 00				1 9 0 0 00	10
11		10	Miscellaneous Expense	C6		2 7 00				2 7 00	11
12		10	✔	T10	✔			2 9 7 00	2 9 7 00		12
13		11	Supplies	C7		7 7 0 00				7 7 0 00	13
14		11	✔	T11	✔			4 9 3 00	4 9 3 00		14
15		12	✔	T12	✔			2 9 4 00	2 9 4 00		15
16		15	Adeline Stein, Drawing	C8		1 2 5 00				1 2 5 00	16
17		15	✔	T15	✔			2 7 5 00	2 7 5 00		17
18		16	Repair Expense	C9		8 8 00				8 8 00	18
19		17	Accts. Rec.—M. Bien	R2			1 2 5 00		1 2 5 00		19
20		17	Supplies	M2		3 4 5 00					20
21			Accts. Pay.—Parks Co.				3 4 5 00				21
22		17	✔	T17	✔			2 0 0 00	2 0 0 00		22
23		18	✔	T18	✔			6 0 0 00	6 0 0 00		23
24		19	✔	T19	✔			1 7 5 00	1 7 5 00		24
25		19	Carried Forward		✔	6 3 3 0 00	10 4 2 0 00	2 8 8 4 00	11 6 3 4 00	4 6 6 0 00	25

JOURNAL PAGE 2

	DATE	ACCOUNT TITLE	DOC. NO.	POST. REF.	GENERAL DEBIT	GENERAL CREDIT	SALES CREDIT	CASH DEBIT	CASH CREDIT	
1	Aug. 19	Brought Forward		✔	6 3 3 0 00	10 4 2 0 00	2 8 8 4 00	11 6 3 4 00	4 6 6 0 00	1
2	22	Supplies	M3		8 0 00					2
3		Accounts Pay.—Parks Co.				8 0 00				3
4	22	✔	T22	✔			4 5 0 00	4 5 0 00		4
5	23	Utilities Expense	C10		5 0 00				5 0 00	5
6	23	Accts. Rec.—M. Bien	S2		4 2 5 00		4 2 5 00			6
7	24	Advertising Expense	C11		8 0 00				8 0 00	7
8	24	✔	T24	✔			2 5 0 00	2 5 0 00		8
9	25	✔	T25	✔			3 2 5 00	3 2 5 00		9
10	26	Supplies	C12		4 5 00				4 5 00	10
11	26	✔	T26	✔			3 1 0 00	3 1 0 00		11
12	29	Accts. Rec.—M. Bien	R3			4 2 5 00		4 2 5 00		12
13	30	Adeline Stein, Drawing	C13		1 5 0 00				1 5 0 00	13
14	31	✔	T31	✔			4 5 0 00	4 5 0 00		14
15	31	Totals			7 1 6 0 00	10 9 2 5 00	5 0 9 4 00	13 8 4 4 00	4 9 8 5 00	15

Prove page 1 of the journal:

Column	Debit Column Totals	Credit Column Totals
General	$ 6,330.00	$10,420.00
Sales		2,884.00
Cash	11,634.00	4,660.00
Totals	$17,964.00	$17,964.00

Prove page 2 of the journal:

Column	Debit Column Totals	Credit Column Totals
General	$ 7,160.00	$10,925.00
Sales		5,094.00
Cash	13,844.00	4,985.00
Totals	$21,004.00	$21,004.00

Prove cash:

Cash on hand at the beginning of the month	$ 0.00
Plus total cash received during the month	13,844.00
Equals Total	13,844.00
Less total cash paid during the month	4,985.00
Equals cash balance at the end of the month	8,859.00
Checkbook balance on the next unused check stub	$ 8,859.00

4-1 RECYCLING PROBLEM, pp. D-3, D-4

Journalizing transactions and posting to a general ledger

2., 5., 6.

JOURNAL   PAGE 1

	DATE	ACCOUNT TITLE	DOC. NO.	POST. REF.	GENERAL DEBIT (1)	GENERAL CREDIT (2)	SALES CREDIT (3)	CASH DEBIT (4)	CASH CREDIT (5)	
1	Aug. 1	Janet Porter, Capital	R1	310		4,500.00		4,500.00		1
2	3	Supplies	C1	130	300.00				300.00	2
3	5	Accts. Rec.—Nicholas Calendo	S1	120	650.00		650.00			3
4	6	✔	T6	✔			630.00	630.00		4
5	9	Utilities Expense	C2	540	130.00				130.00	5
6	11	Rent Expense	C3	530	530.00				530.00	6
7	13	Supplies	M1	130	800.00					7
8		Accts. Pay.—Jordan Supplies		210		800.00				8
9	13	✔	T13	✔			650.00	650.00		9
10	16	Miscellaneous Expense	C4	520	55.00				55.00	10
11	18	Accts. Pay.—Jordan Supplies	C5	210	500.00				500.00	11
12	20	Supplies	C6	130	105.00				105.00	12
13	20	Accts. Rec.—Nicholas Calendo	R2	120		350.00		350.00		13
14	25	Advertising Expense	C7	510	250.00				250.00	14
15	27	Supplies	C8	130	75.00				75.00	15
16	27	✔	T27	✔			1,200.00	1,200.00		16
17	30	Janet Porter, Drawing	C9	320	800.00				800.00	17
18	31	✔	T31	✔			780.00	780.00		18
19	31	Totals			4,195.00	5,650.00	3,910.00	8,110.00	2,745.00	19
20					(✔)	(✔)	(410)	(110)	(110)	20

3. *Prove the journal:*

Column	Debit Column Totals	Credit Column Totals
General	$ 4,195.00	$ 5,650.00
Sales		3,910.00
Cash	8,110.00	2,745.00
Totals	$12,305.00	$12,305.00

4. *Prove cash:*

Cash on hand at the beginning of the month	$ 0.00
Plus total cash received during the month	8,110.00
Equals Total	8,110.00
Less total cash paid during the month	2,745.00
Equals cash balance at the end of the month	5,365.00
Checkbook balance on the next unused check stub	$5,365.00

1., 6. **GENERAL LEDGER**

ACCOUNT Cash ACCOUNT NO. 110

DATE		ITEM	POST. REF.	DEBIT	CREDIT	BALANCE	
						DEBIT	CREDIT
20-- Aug.	31		1	8 1 1 0 00		8 1 1 0 00	
	31		1		2 7 4 5 00	5 3 6 5 00	

ACCOUNT Accounts Receivable—Nicholas Calendo ACCOUNT NO. 120

DATE		ITEM	POST. REF.	DEBIT	CREDIT	BALANCE	
						DEBIT	CREDIT
20-- Aug.	5		1	6 5 0 00		6 5 0 00	
	20		1		3 5 0 00	3 0 0 00	

ACCOUNT Supplies ACCOUNT NO. 130

DATE		ITEM	POST. REF.	DEBIT	CREDIT	BALANCE	
						DEBIT	CREDIT
20-- Aug.	3		1	3 0 0 00		3 0 0 00	
	13		1	8 0 0 00		1 1 0 0 00	
	20		1	1 0 5 00		1 2 0 5 00	
	27		1	7 5 00		1 2 8 0 00	

ACCOUNT Accounts Payable—Jordan Supplies ACCOUNT NO. 210

DATE		ITEM	POST. REF.	DEBIT	CREDIT	BALANCE	
						DEBIT	CREDIT
20-- Aug.	13		1		8 0 0 00		8 0 0 00
	18		1	5 0 0 00			3 0 0 00

ACCOUNT Janet Porter, Capital ACCOUNT NO. 310

DATE		ITEM	POST. REF.	DEBIT	CREDIT	BALANCE	
						DEBIT	CREDIT
20-- Aug.	1		1		4 5 0 0 00		4 5 0 0 00

4-1 RECYCLING PROBLEM (concluded)

1., 6.   **GENERAL LEDGER**

ACCOUNT Janet Porter, Drawing   ACCOUNT NO. 320

DATE	ITEM	POST. REF.	DEBIT	CREDIT	BALANCE DEBIT	BALANCE CREDIT
20-- Aug. 30		1	8 0 0 00		8 0 0 00	

ACCOUNT Sales   ACCOUNT NO. 410

DATE	ITEM	POST. REF.	DEBIT	CREDIT	BALANCE DEBIT	BALANCE CREDIT
20-- Aug. 31		1		3 9 1 0 00		3 9 1 0 00

ACCOUNT Advertising Expense   ACCOUNT NO. 510

DATE	ITEM	POST. REF.	DEBIT	CREDIT	BALANCE DEBIT	BALANCE CREDIT
20-- Aug. 25		1	2 5 0 00		2 5 0 00	

ACCOUNT Miscellaneous Expense   ACCOUNT NO. 520

DATE	ITEM	POST. REF.	DEBIT	CREDIT	BALANCE DEBIT	BALANCE CREDIT
20-- Aug. 16		1	5 5 00		5 5 00	

ACCOUNT Rent Expense   ACCOUNT NO. 530

DATE	ITEM	POST. REF.	DEBIT	CREDIT	BALANCE DEBIT	BALANCE CREDIT
20-- Aug. 11		1	5 3 0 00		5 3 0 00	

ACCOUNT *Utilities Expense*   ACCOUNT NO. **540**

DATE	ITEM	POST. REF.	DEBIT	CREDIT	BALANCE DEBIT	BALANCE CREDIT
20-- Aug. 9		1	1 3 0 00		1 3 0 00	

5-1 RECYCLING PROBLEM, p. D-4

Reconciling a bank statement; journalizing a bank service charge, a dishonored check, and petty cash transactions

1., 3.

JOURNAL   PAGE 12

	DATE	ACCOUNT TITLE	DOC. NO.	POST. REF.	GENERAL DEBIT	GENERAL CREDIT	SALES CREDIT	CASH DEBIT	CASH CREDIT	
1	20-- May 21	Petty Cash	C51		1 5 0 00				1 5 0 00	1
2	24	Supplies	C52		7 2 00				7 2 00	2
3	26	Repair Expense	C53		8 5 00				8 5 00	3
4	27	Accts. Rec.—Corner Cafe	M22		9 5 00				9 5 00	4
5	28	Miscellaneous Expense	C54		4 2 00				4 2 00	5
6	31	Tao Vang, Drawing	C55		2 0 0 00				2 0 0 00	6
7	31	Supplies	C56		8 5 00				1 0 5 00	7
8		Miscellaneous Expense			2 0 00					8
9	31	Miscellaneous Expense	M23		2 5 00				2 5 00	9
10										10
11										11
12										12

2.

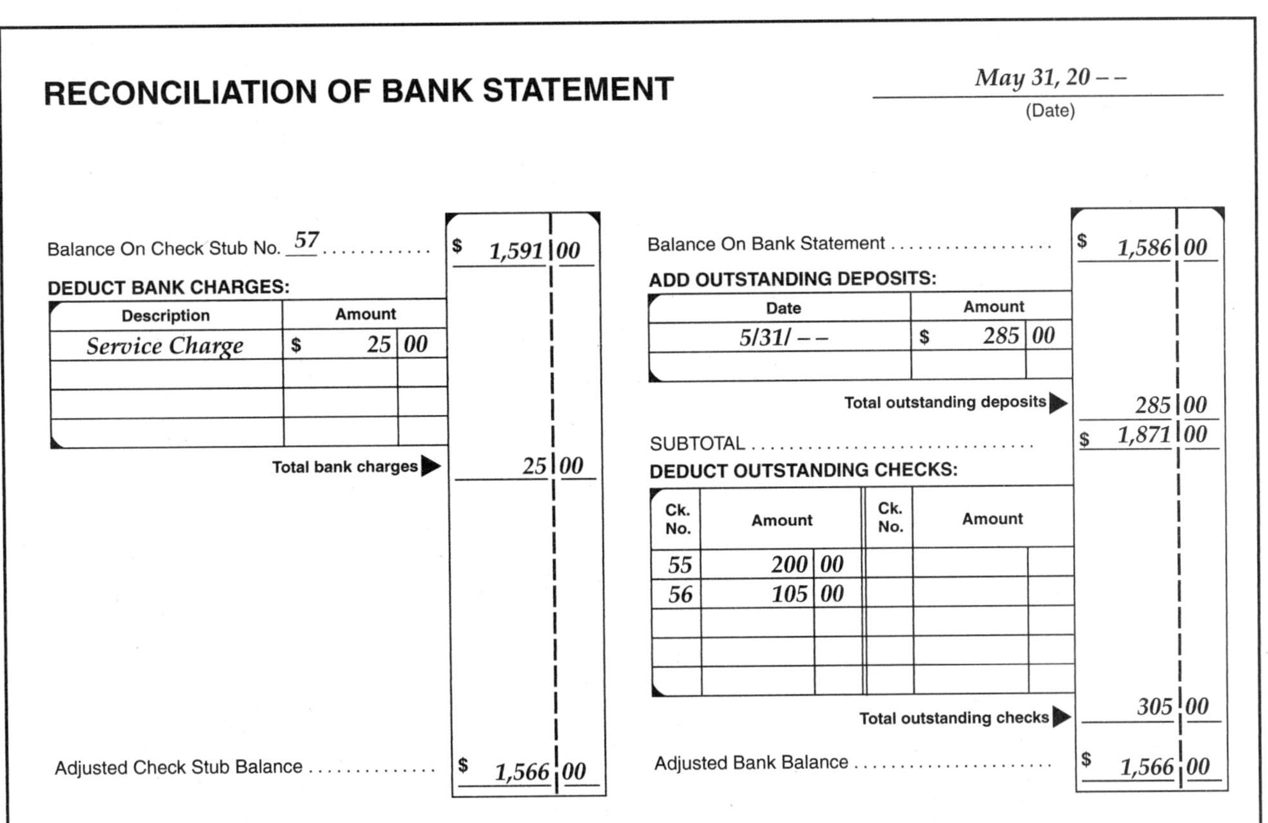

RECONCILIATION OF BANK STATEMENT   *May 31, 20 – –*
(Date)

Balance On Check Stub No. 57 .... $ 1,591 | 00

DEDUCT BANK CHARGES:

Description	Amount
Service Charge	$ 25 00

Total bank charges ▶ 25 | 00

Adjusted Check Stub Balance .... $ 1,566 | 00

Balance On Bank Statement .... $ 1,586 | 00

ADD OUTSTANDING DEPOSITS:

Date	Amount
5/31/ – –	$ 285 00

Total outstanding deposits ▶ 285 | 00

SUBTOTAL .... $ 1,871 | 00

DEDUCT OUTSTANDING CHECKS:

Ck. No.	Amount	Ck. No.	Amount
55	200 00		
56	105 00		

Total outstanding checks ▶ 305 | 00

Adjusted Bank Balance .... $ 1,566 | 00

6-1 RECYCLING PROBLEM, p. D-5

Completing a work sheet

1., 2., 3., 4., 5., 6.

Hibbing Hair Care

Work Sheet

For Month Ended February 28, 20 – –

ACCOUNT TITLE	TRIAL BALANCE		ADJUSTMENTS		INCOME STATEMENT		BALANCE SHEET	
	DEBIT	CREDIT	DEBIT	CREDIT	DEBIT	CREDIT	DEBIT	CREDIT
1 Cash	2609 00						2609 00	
2 Petty Cash	300 00						300 00	
3 Accts. Rec.—Robert Perpich	581 00						581 00	
4 Supplies	895 00			(a) 445 00			450 00	
5 Prepaid Insurance	1200 00			(b) 200 00			1000 00	
6 Accts. Pay.—Ely Supplies		450 00						450 00
7 Jens Miller-Smith, Capital		4550 00						4550 00
8 Jens Miller-Smith, Drawing	300 00						300 00	
9 Income Summary								
10 Sales		3100 00				3100 00		
11 Advertising Expense	425 00				425 00			
12 Insurance Expense			(b) 200 00		200 00			
13 Miscellaneous Expense	250 00				250 00			
14 Rent Expense	1100 00				1100 00			
15 Supplies Expense			(a) 445 00		445 00			
16 Utilities Expense	440 00				440 00			
17	8100 00	8100 00	645 00	645 00	2860 00	3100 00	5240 00	5000 00
18 Net Income					240 00			240 00
19					3100 00	3100 00	5240 00	5240 00

7-1 RECYCLING PROBLEM, p. D-6

Preparing financial statements

1., 2.

SuperClean

Income Statement

For Month Ended August 31, 20 – –

		% OF SALES
Revenue:		
Sales	5 8 8 1 00	100.0
Expenses:		
Advertising Expense	6 2 5 00	
Insurance Expense	1 5 0 00	
Miscellaneous Expense	1 4 5 00	
Supplies Expense	9 2 5 00	
Utilities Expense	1 3 7 1 00	
Total Expenses	3 2 1 6 00	54.7
Net Income	2 6 6 5 00	45.3

3.

SuperClean

Balance Sheet

August 31, 20 – –

Assets		Liabilities	
Cash	5 6 3 2 00	Accts. Pay.—DV Supply	5 9 3 00
Accts. Rec.—D. Dawson	1 7 5 00	Accts. Pay.—Supply Warehouse	7 0 0 00
Accts. Rec.—K. Keene	3 1 5 00	Total Liabilities	1 2 9 3 00
Supplies	4 6 7 00	**Owner's Equity**	
Prepaid Insurance	9 0 0 00	Michelle Delist, Capital	6 1 9 6 00
Total Assets	7 4 8 9 00	Total Liab. and Owner's Equity	7 4 8 9 00

8-1 RECYCLING PROBLEM, p. D-7

Journalizing adjusting and closing entries

1., 2.

JOURNAL   PAGE 16

	DATE		ACCOUNT TITLE	DOC. NO.	POST. REF.	GENERAL DEBIT	GENERAL CREDIT	SALES CREDIT	CASH DEBIT	CASH CREDIT	
1			*Adjusting Entries*								1
2	20-- Aug.	31	Supplies Expense			9 2 5 00					2
3			Supplies				9 2 5 00				3
4		31	Insurance Expense			1 5 0 00					4
5			Prepaid Insurance				1 5 0 00				5
6			*Closing Entries*								6
7		31	Sales			5 8 8 1 00					7
8			Income Summary				5 8 8 1 00				8
9		31	Income Summary			3 2 1 6 00					9
10			Advertising Expense				6 2 5 00				10
11			Insurance Expense				1 5 0 00				11
12			Miscellaneous Expense				1 4 5 00				12
13			Supplies Expense				9 2 5 00				13
14			Utilities Expense				1 3 7 1 00				14
15		31	Income Summary			2 6 6 5 00					15
16			Michelle Delist, Capital				2 6 6 5 00				16
17		31	Michelle Delist, Capital			1 5 0 0 00					17
18			Michelle Delist, Drawing				1 5 0 0 00				18
19											19
20											20
21											21
22											22

9-1 RECYCLING PROBLEM, pp. D-7, D-8

Journalizing purchases, cash payments, and other transactions

1., 5.

PURCHASES JOURNAL   PAGE 9

	DATE		ACCOUNT CREDITED	PURCH. NO.	POST. REF.	PURCHASES DR. ACCTS. PAY. CR.	
1	20-- Aug.	9	*Peterson Sports*	445		3 5 6 0 00	1
2		22	*Camo Clothing*	446		4 0 5 0 00	2
3		31	*Total*			7 6 1 0 00	3
4							4
5							5
6							6
7							7
8							8
9							9
10							10
11							11
12							12

1., 2.

CASH PAYMENTS JOURNAL

PAGE 15

	DATE		ACCOUNT TITLE	CK. NO.	POST. REF.	GENERAL DEBIT	GENERAL CREDIT	ACCOUNTS PAYABLE DEBIT	PURCHASES DISCOUNT CREDIT	CASH CREDIT	
						1	2	3	4	5	
1	20-- Aug.	1	Rent Expense	772		1 000 00				1 000 00	1
2		2	Advertising Expense	773		720 00				720 00	2
3		4	Arrowhead Supply	774				4 210 00		4 210 00	3
4		6	Utilities Expense	775		420 00				420 00	4
5		7	Johnson Office Supply	776				420 00	8 40	411 60	5
6		9	Supplies—Store	777		224 00				224 00	6
7		11	Purchases	778		1 392 00				1 392 00	7
8		13	Purchases	779		495 00				495 00	8
9		15	Peterson Sports	780				3 327 00	66 54	3 260 46	9
10		20	Purchases	781		156 00				156 00	10
11		21	Evans Sports Corporation	782				1 950 00		1 950 00	11
12		24	Supplies—Store	783		245 00				245 00	12
13		29	Purchases	784		1 154 00				1 154 00	13
14		29	Carried Forward		✔	5 806 00		9 907 00	74 94	15 638 06	14
15											15

2.

Column Title	Debit Column Totals	Credit Column Totals
General Debit	$ 5,806.00	
General Credit		$ —
Accounts Payable Debit	9,907.00	
Purchases Discount Credit		74.94
Cash Credit		15,638.06
Totals	$15,713.00	$15,713.00

9-1 RECYCLING PROBLEM (continued)

3., 4., 6., 7.

CASH PAYMENTS JOURNAL
PAGE 16

	DATE	ACCOUNT TITLE	CK. NO.	POST. REF.	GENERAL DEBIT	GENERAL CREDIT	ACCOUNTS PAYABLE DEBIT	PURCHASES DISCOUNT CREDIT	CASH CREDIT	
1	Aug. 29	Brought Forward		✔	5 8 0 6 00		9 9 0 7 00	74 94	15 6 3 8 06	1
2	31	Camo Clothing	785				4 0 5 0 00	81 00	3 9 6 9 00	2
3	31	Supplies—Office	786		2 5 66				1 2 7 80	3
4		Supplies—Store			4 8 25					4
5		Miscellaneous Expense			5 4 33					5
6		Cash Short and Over				0 44				6
7					5 9 3 4 24	0 44	13 9 5 7 00	1 5 5 94	19 7 3 4 86	7
8										8

6.

Column Title	Debit Column Totals	Credit Column Totals
General Debit	$ 5,934.24	
General Credit		$ 0.44
Accounts Payable Debit	13,957.00	
Purchases Discount Credit		155.94
Cash Credit		19,734.86
Totals	$19,891.24	$19,891.24

1.

GENERAL JOURNAL

PAGE 12

	DATE		ACCOUNT TITLE	DOC. NO.	POST. REF.	DEBIT	CREDIT	
1	Aug. 20--	3	Supplies—Office	M62		4 2 0 00		1
2			Accounts Pay./Johnson Office Supply				4 2 0 00	2
3		13	Accounts Pay./Peterson Sports	DM19		2 3 3 00		3
4			Purchases Returns and Allow.				2 3 3 00	4
5		15	Accounts Pay./Evans Sports Corporation	DM20		1 1 2 00		5
6			Purchases Returns and Allow.				1 1 2 00	6
7		23	Supplies—Store	M63		1 2 0 00		7
8			Accounts Pay./Mancil Marketing				1 2 0 00	8
9								9
10								10
11								11
12								12
13								13
14								14
15								15

10-1 RECYCLING PROBLEM, pp. D-8, D-9

Journalizing sales and cash receipts transactions; proving and ruling journals

1.

GENERAL JOURNAL   PAGE 17

	DATE	ACCOUNT TITLE	DOC. NO.	POST. REF.	DEBIT	CREDIT	
1	Nov. 29	Sales Returns and Allowances	CM43		1 8 2 0 00		1
2		Sales Tax Payable			1 0 9 20		2
3		Accounts Receivable/Davis Construction		/		1 9 2 9 20	3
4							4
5							5
6							6
7							7
8							8
9							9
10							10
11							11
12							12
13							13
14							14
15							15
16							16
17							17
18							18
19							19
20							20
21							21
22							22
23							23
24							24
25							25

1., 2., 3.

SALES JOURNAL PAGE 22

	DATE	ACCOUNT DEBITED	SALE NO.	POST. REF.	1 ACCOUNTS RECEIVABLE DEBIT	2 SALES CREDIT	3 SALES TAX PAYABLE CREDIT	
1	20-- Nov. 24	Brought Forward		✔	15 996 55	15 148 25	8 48 30	1
2	28	Margaret Sienna	889		7 03 84	6 64 00	3 9 84	2
3	30	State University	890		2 118 00	2 118 00		3
4	30	Totals			18 818 39	17 930 25	8 88 14	4
5								5
6								6
7								7
8								8
9								9
10								10
11								11
12								12
13								13
14								14
15								15
16								16
17								17
18								18

2.

Col. No.	Column Title	Debit Totals	Credit Totals
1	Accounts Receivable Debit	$18,818.39	
2	Sales Credit		$17,930.25
3	Sales Tax Payable Credit		888.14
	Totals	$18,818.39	$18,818.39

10-1 RECYCLING PROBLEM (concluded)

1., 4., 6.

CASH RECEIPTS JOURNAL   PAGE 23

	DATE	ACCOUNT TITLE	DOC. NO.	POST. REF.	GENERAL DEBIT (1)	GENERAL CREDIT (2)	ACCOUNTS RECEIVABLE CREDIT (3)	SALES CREDIT (4)	SALES TAX PAYABLE CREDIT (5)	SALES DISCOUNT DEBIT (6)	CASH DEBIT (7)	
1	20-- Nov. 24	Brought Forward		✔			13 484 25	25 118 77	1 507 13		40 084 90	1
2	25	Davis Construction	R334				1 408 00			28 16	1 379 84	2
3	26	✔	TS38	✔				4 844 00	290 64		5 134 64	3
4	28	Ventura Fencing	R335				2 849 00				2 849 00	4
5	30	✔	TS39	✔				839 00	50 34		889 34	5
6	30	Totals					17 741 25	30 801 77	1 848 11	53 41	50 337 72	6
7												7
8												8
9												9
10												10
11												11
12												12
13												13
14												14

4.

Col. No.	Column Title	Debit Totals	Credit Totals
1	General Debit	$ —	
2	General Credit		$ —
3	Accounts Receivable Credit		17,741.25
4	Sales Credit		30,801.77
5	Sales Tax Payable Credit		1,848.11
6	Sales Discount Debit	53.41	
7	Cash Debit	50,337.72	
	Totals	$50,391.13	$50,391.13

5.

CASH PROOF

Cash on hand at the beginning of the month	$ 8,483.31
Plus total cash received during the month	50,337.72
Equals total	$58,821.03
Less total cash paid during the month	42,194.33
Equals cash balance on hand at end of the month	$16,626.70
Checkbook balance on the next unused check stub	$16,626.70

11-1 RECYCLING PROBLEM, p. D-9

Posting to general and subsidiary ledgers

1., 2.

SALES JOURNAL   PAGE 9

	DATE	ACCOUNT DEBITED	SALE NO.	POST. REF.	1 ACCOUNTS RECEIVABLE DEBIT	2 SALES CREDIT	3 SALES TAX PAYABLE CREDIT	
1	Aug. 14	Joe Chapin	50	120	3 8 2 20	3 6 4 00	1 8 20	1
2	15	Susan King	51	130	1 8 3 75	1 7 5 00	8 75	2
3	24	Gary Voyles	52	140	1 9 8 45	1 8 9 00	9 45	3
4	25	Joan Aberg	53	110	1 3 9 65	1 3 3 00	6 65	4
5	31	*Totals*			9 0 4 05	8 6 1 00	4 3 05	5
6					(1130)	(4110)	(2120)	6

1., 3.

PURCHASES JOURNAL   PAGE 9

	DATE	ACCOUNT CREDITED	PURCH. NO.	POST. REF.	PURCHASES DR. ACCTS. PAY. CR.	
1	Aug. 2	Diamond T. Boots	63	220	2 3 1 0 00	1
2	18	Boot Town	64	210	1 3 1 6 00	2
3	31	Western Leather Co.	65	240	1 2 0 4 00	3
4	31	*Total*			4 8 3 0 00	4
5					(5110) (2110)	5
6						6

1.

GENERAL JOURNAL

PAGE 9

	DATE		ACCOUNT TITLE	DOC. NO.	POST. REF.	DEBIT	CREDIT	
1	Aug.	9	Supplies—Office	M30	*1145*	1 8 9 00		1
2			Accounts Payable/National Supply		2110/230		1 8 9 00	2
3		25	Sales Returns and Allowances	CM11	*4130*	1 0 0 00		3
4			Sales Tax Payable		*2120*	5 00		4
5			Accounts Receivable/Joe Chapin		1130/120		1 0 5 00	5
6		27	Accounts Payable/Diamond T. Boots	DM5	2110/220	4 2 1 00		6
7			Purchases Returns and Allow.		*5130*		4 2 1 00	7
8								8
9								9

11-1 RECYCLING PROBLEM (continued)

1., 4.

CASH RECEIPTS JOURNAL

PAGE 9

	DATE		ACCOUNT TITLE	DOC. NO.	POST. REF.	GENERAL		ACCOUNTS RECEIVABLE CREDIT	SALES CREDIT	SALES TAX PAYABLE CREDIT	SALES DISCOUNT DEBIT	CASH DEBIT	
						DEEIT	CREDIT						
						1	2	3	4	5	6	7	
1	Aug.	4	Gary Voyles	R29	140			3 6 7 50				3 6 7 50	1
2		5	✔	TS28	✔				4 6 9 0 00	2 3 4 50		4 9 2 4 50	2
3		12	✔	TS29	✔				5 7 9 6 00	2 8 9 80		6 0 8 5 80	3
4		19	✔	TS30	✔				5 7 1 2 00	2 8 5 60		5 9 9 7 60	4
5		26	✔	TS31	✔				6 3 4 2 00	3 1 7 10		6 6 5 9 10	5
6		28	Joan Aberg	R30	110			2 4 9 90				2 4 9 90	6
7		31	✔	TS32	✔				3 6 6 8 00	1 8 3 40		3 8 5 1 40	7
8		31	Totals					6 1 7 40	26 2 0 8 00	1 3 1 0 40		28 1 3 5 80	8
9								(1130)	(4110)	(2120)		(1110)	9
10													10
11													11
12													12
13													13
14													14

1., 5.

CASH PAYMENTS JOURNAL

PAGE 9

	DATE		ACCOUNT TITLE	CK. NO.	POST. REF.	GENERAL DEBIT (1)	GENERAL CREDIT (2)	ACCOUNTS PAYABLE DEBIT (3)	PURCHASES DISCOUNT CREDIT (4)	CASH CREDIT (5)	
1	20-- Aug.	1	Rent Expense	782	6145	1 3 0 0 00				1 3 0 0 00	1
2		7	Utilities Expense	783	6170	2 2 1 34				2 2 1 34	2
3		10	Western Leather Co.	784	240			3 2 7 6 00		3 2 7 6 00	3
4		15	Yeatman Corporation	785	250			3 5 0 0 00	7 0 00	3 4 3 0 00	4
5		28	Boot Town	786	210			2 0 7 2 00		2 0 7 2 00	5
6		31	Supplies—Office	787	1145	5 8 80				2 8 2 10	6
7			Supplies—Store	788	1150	8 0 50					7
8			Advertising Expense	789	6105	8 9 60					8
9			Miscellaneous Expense	790	6135	5 3 15					9
10			Cash Short and Over		6110	0 05					10
11		31	Totals			1 8 0 3 44	———	8 8 4 8 00	7 0 00	10 5 8 1 44	11
12						(✓)		(2110)	(5120)	(1110)	12
13											13
14											14
15											15

11-1 RECYCLING PROBLEM (continued)

1., 6.
ACCOUNTS RECEIVABLE LEDGER

CUSTOMER Joan Aberg CUSTOMER NO. 110

DATE		ITEM	POST. REF.	DEBIT	CREDIT	DEBIT BALANCE
Aug.	1	Balance	✔			2 4 9 90
	25		S9	1 3 9 65		3 8 9 55
	28		CR9		2 4 9 90	1 3 9 65

CUSTOMER Joe Chapin CUSTOMER NO. 120

DATE		ITEM	POST. REF.	DEBIT	CREDIT	DEBIT BALANCE
Aug.	14		S9	3 8 2 20		3 8 2 20
	25		G9		1 0 5 00	2 7 7 20

CUSTOMER Susan King CUSTOMER NO. 130

DATE		ITEM	POST. REF.	DEBIT	CREDIT	DEBIT BALANCE
Aug.	15		S9	1 8 3 75		1 8 3 75

CUSTOMER Gary Voyles CUSTOMER NO. 140

DATE		ITEM	POST. REF.	DEBIT	CREDIT	DEBIT BALANCE
Aug.	1	Balance	✔			3 6 7 50
	24		S9	1 9 8 45		5 6 5 95
	4		CR9		3 6 7 50	1 9 8 45

1., 6.   **ACCOUNTS PAYABLE LEDGER**

VENDOR Boot Town   VENDOR NO. 210

DATE		ITEM	POST. REF.	DEBIT	CREDIT	CREDIT BALANCE
Aug.	1	Balance	✓			2 0 7 2 00
	18		P9		1 3 1 6 00	3 3 8 8 00
	28		CP9	2 0 7 2 00		1 3 1 6 00

VENDOR Diamond T. Boots   VENDOR NO. 220

DATE		ITEM	POST. REF.	DEBIT	CREDIT	CREDIT BALANCE
Aug.	2		P9		2 3 1 0 00	2 3 1 0 00
	27		G9	4 2 1 00		1 8 8 9 00

VENDOR National Supply   VENDOR NO. 230

DATE		ITEM	POST. REF.	DEBIT	CREDIT	CREDIT BALANCE
Aug.	9		G9		1 8 9 00	1 8 9 00

VENDOR Western Leather Co.   VENDOR NO. 240

DATE		ITEM	POST. REF.	DEBIT	CREDIT	CREDIT BALANCE
Aug.	1	Balance	✓			3 2 7 6 00
	31		P9		1 2 0 4 00	4 4 8 0 00
	10		CP9	3 2 7 6 00		1 2 0 4 00

VENDOR Yeatman Corporation   VENDOR NO. 250

DATE		ITEM	POST. REF.	DEBIT	CREDIT	CREDIT BALANCE
Aug.	1	Balance	✓			3 5 0 0 00
	15		CP9	3 5 0 0 00		—

11-1 **RECYCLING PROBLEM (continued)**

6.

Custom Boots

Schedule of Accounts Receivable

August 31, 20 – –

Joan Aberg	139	65
Joe Chapin	277	20
Susan King	183	75
Gary Voyles	198	45
Total Accounts Receivable	799	05

Custom Boots

Schedule of Accounts Payable

August 31, 20 – –

Boot Town	1316	00
Diamond T. Boots	1889	00
National Supply	189	00
Western Leather Co.	1204	00
Total Accounts Payable	4598	00

1., 2., 3., 4., 5., 6. **GENERAL LEDGER**

ACCOUNT Cash ACCOUNT NO. 1110

DATE		ITEM	POST. REF.	DEBIT	CREDIT	BALANCE	
						DEBIT	CREDIT
Aug. 20--	1	Balance	✔			15 840 00	
	31		CR9	28 135 80		43 975 80	
	31		CP9		10 581 44	33 394 36	

ACCOUNT Accounts Receivable ACCOUNT NO. 1130

DATE		ITEM	POST. REF.	DEBIT	CREDIT	BALANCE	
						DEBIT	CREDIT
Aug. 20--	1	Balance	✔			617 40	
	25		G9		105 00	512 40	
	31		S9	904 05		1 416 45	
	31		CR9		617 40	799 05	

ACCOUNT Supplies—Office ACCOUNT NO. 1145

DATE		ITEM	POST. REF.	DEBIT	CREDIT	BALANCE	
						DEBIT	CREDIT
Aug. 20--	1	Balance	✔			2 196 00	
	9		G9	189 00		2 385 00	
	31		CP9	58 80		2 443 80	

ACCOUNT Supplies—Store ACCOUNT NO. 1150

DATE		ITEM	POST. REF.	DEBIT	CREDIT	BALANCE	
						DEBIT	CREDIT
Aug. 20--	1	Balance	✔			1 872 00	
	31		CP9	80 50		1 952 50	

ACCOUNT Accounts Payable ACCOUNT NO. 2110

DATE		ITEM	POST. REF.	DEBIT	CREDIT	BALANCE	
						DEBIT	CREDIT
Aug. 20--	1	Balance	✔				8 848 00
	9		G9		189 00		9 037 00
	27		G9	421 00			8 616 00
	31		P9		4 830 00		13 446 00
	31		CP9	8 848 00			4 598 00

11-1   RECYCLING PROBLEM (continued)

ACCOUNT Sales Tax Payable   ACCOUNT NO. 2120

DATE		ITEM	POST. REF.	DEBIT	CREDIT	BALANCE DEBIT	BALANCE CREDIT
20-- Aug.	1	Balance	✔				1 1 2 5 00
	25		G9	5 00			1 1 2 0 00
	31		S9		4 3 05		1 1 6 3 05
	31		CR9		1 3 1 0 40		2 4 7 3 45

ACCOUNT Sales   ACCOUNT NO. 4110

DATE		ITEM	POST. REF.	DEBIT	CREDIT	BALANCE DEBIT	BALANCE CREDIT
20-- Aug.	1	Balance	✔				180 0 0 0 00
	31		S9		8 6 1 00		180 8 6 1 00
	31		CR9		26 2 0 8 00		207 0 6 9 00

ACCOUNT Sales Returns and Allowances   ACCOUNT NO. 4130

DATE		ITEM	POST. REF.	DEBIT	CREDIT	BALANCE DEBIT	BALANCE CREDIT
20-- Aug.	1	Balance	✔			1 5 1 8 11	
	25		G9	1 0 0 00		1 6 1 8 11	

ACCOUNT Purchases   ACCOUNT NO. 5110

DATE		ITEM	POST. REF.	DEBIT	CREDIT	BALANCE DEBIT	BALANCE CREDIT
20-- Aug.	1	Balance	✔			105 6 0 0 00	
	31		P9	4 8 3 0 00		110 4 3 0 00	

ACCOUNT Purchases Discount   ACCOUNT NO. 5120

DATE		ITEM	POST. REF.	DEBIT	CREDIT	BALANCE DEBIT	BALANCE CREDIT
20-- Aug.	1	Balance	✔				2 1 1 0 50
	31		CP9		7 0 00		2 1 8 0 50

ACCOUNT Purchases Returns and Allowances   ACCOUNT NO. 5130

DATE		ITEM	POST. REF.	DEBIT	CREDIT	BALANCE DEBIT	BALANCE CREDIT
Aug. 20--	1	Balance	✔				1 5 4 8 00
	27		G9		4 2 1 00		1 9 6 9 00

ACCOUNT Advertising Expense   ACCOUNT NO. 6105

DATE		ITEM	POST. REF.	DEBIT	CREDIT	BALANCE DEBIT	BALANCE CREDIT
Aug. 20--	1	Balance	✔			2 7 7 0 00	
	31		CP9	8 9 60		2 8 5 9 60	

ACCOUNT Cash Short and Over   ACCOUNT NO. 6110

DATE		ITEM	POST. REF.	DEBIT	CREDIT	BALANCE DEBIT	BALANCE CREDIT
Aug. 20--	1	Balance	✔			1 4 11	
	31		CP9	0 05		1 4 16	

ACCOUNT Miscellaneous Expense   ACCOUNT NO. 6135

DATE		ITEM	POST. REF.	DEBIT	CREDIT	BALANCE DEBIT	BALANCE CREDIT
Aug. 20--	1	Balance	✔			1 5 2 0 00	
	31		CP9	5 3 15		1 5 7 3 15	

ACCOUNT Rent Expense   ACCOUNT NO. 6145

DATE		ITEM	POST. REF.	DEBIT	CREDIT	BALANCE DEBIT	BALANCE CREDIT
Aug. 20--	1	Balance	✔			9 1 0 0 00	
	1		CP9	1 3 0 0 00		10 4 0 0 00	

ACCOUNT Utilities Expense   ACCOUNT NO. 6170

DATE		ITEM	POST. REF.	DEBIT	CREDIT	BALANCE DEBIT	BALANCE CREDIT
Aug. 20--	1	Balance	✔			2 2 6 0 00	
	7		CP9	2 2 1 34		2 4 8 1 34	

12-1 RECYCLING PROBLEM, pp. D-9, D-10

Preparing a semimonthly payroll

1.

PAYROLL REGISTER

SEMIMONTHLY PERIOD ENDED July 31, 20 – –   DATE OF PAYMENT July 31, 20 – –

					1	2	3	4	5	6	7	8	9	10	
				EARNINGS				**DEDUCTIONS**							
EMPL. NO.	EMPLOYEE'S NAME	MARI-TAL STATUS	NO. OF ALLOW-ANCES		REGULAR	OVERTIME	TOTAL	FEDERAL INCOME TAX	SOC. SEC. TAX	MEDICARE TAX	HEALTH INSURANCE	OTHER	TOTAL	NET PAY	CHECK NO.
5	Abrams, Thomas	S	1		8920 00		8920 00	83 00	55 30	12 93	35 00		186 23	705 77	558
6	Carroll, John	M	2		8800 00	90 00	9700 00	38 00	60 14	14 07	60 00		172 21	797 79	
1	Harris, Jonathan	S	1		9240 00		9240 00	89 00	57 29	13 40	35 00		194 69	729 31	
4	Kennard, Mary	S	1		10560 00	72 00	11280 00	119 00	69 94	16 36	35 00		240 30	887 70	
2	Locke, Anna	M	2		9940 00		9940 00	40 00	61 63	14 41	60 00		176 04	817 96	562
7	Rayford, Stan	M	2		8120 00		8120 00	22 00	50 34	11 77	60 00		144 11	667 89	
3	Suell, Nicole	M	3		8600 00		8600 00	15 00	53 32	12 47	80 00		160 79	699 21	
	Totals				64180 00	162 00	65800 00	406 00	407 96	95 41	365 00		1274 37	5305 63	

12-1 RECYCLING PROBLEM (concluded)

2., 3.

NO. 621
Date: 7/31 20-- $ 5,305.63
To: Payroll Account
982-561-4732
For: Payroll for July 16-31

BAL. BRO'T. FOR'D	11,530.50
AMT. DEPOSITED	
TOTAL	11,530.50
AMT. THIS CHECK	5,305.63
BAL. CAR'D. FOR'D	6,224.87

GENERAL ACCOUNT NO. **621** 66-877/530

SANFORD COMPANY

July 31, 20 --

PAY TO THE ORDER OF Payroll Account 982-561-4732 $ 5,305.63

Five thousand three hundred five and 63/100 DOLLARS

For Classroom Use Only

Peoples Bank and Trust
Charlotte, NC 28206-8444

Student's Name

⑆053008774⑆ 196⑈2236⑈42⑈

CHECK NO. **558**

PERIOD ENDING	7 / 31 / 20--
EARNINGS	$ 892.00
REG.	$ 892.00
O.T.	$ —0—
DEDUCTIONS	$ 186.23
INC. TAX	$ 83.00
SOC. SEC. TAX	$ 55.30
MED. TAX	$ 12.93
HEALTH INS.	$ 35.00
OTHER	$ —0—
NET PAY	$ 705.77

PAYROLL ACCOUNT 66-877/530

July 31, 20 --

NO. **558**

PAY TO THE ORDER OF Thomas Abrams $ 705.77

Seven hundred five and 77/100 DOLLARS

For Classroom Use Only

Peoples Bank and Trust
Charlotte, NC 28206-8444

SANFORD COMPANY
Student's Name

⑆053008774⑆ 982⑈561⑈4732

CHECK NO. **562**

PERIOD ENDING	7 / 31 / 20--
EARNINGS	$ 994.00
REG.	$ 994.00
O.T.	$ —0—
DEDUCTIONS	$ 176.04
INC. TAX	$ 40.00
SOC. SEC. TAX	$ 61.63
MED. TAX	$ 14.41
HEALTH INS.	$ 60.00
OTHER	$ —0—
NET PAY	$ 817.96

PAYROLL ACCOUNT 66-877/530

July 31, 20 --

NO. **562**

PAY TO THE ORDER OF Anna Locke $ 817.96

Eight hundred seventeen and 96/100 DOLLARS

For Classroom Use Only

Peoples Bank and Trust
Charlotte, NC 28206-8444

SANFORD COMPANY
Student's Name

⑆053008774⑆ 982⑈561⑈4732

13-1 RECYCLING PROBLEM, p. D-10

Journalizing payroll transactions

1.

GENERAL JOURNAL   PAGE 10

	DATE		ACCOUNT TITLE	DOC. NO.	POST. REF.	DEBIT	CREDIT	
1	20-- Jan.	31	Payroll Taxes Expense	M24		8 1 9 92		1
2			Social Security Tax Payable				3 6 7 04	2
3			Medicare Tax Payable				8 5 84	3
4			Unemployment Tax Payable—Federal				4 7 36	4
5			Unemployment Tax Payable—State				3 1 9 68	5
6	Feb.	28	Payroll Taxes Expense	M28		8 3 9 03		6
7			Social Security Tax Payable				3 7 5 60	7
8			Medicare Tax Payable				8 7 84	8
9			Unemployment Tax Payable—Federal				4 8 46	9
10			Unemployment Tax Payable—State				3 2 7 13	10
11	Mar.	31	Payroll Taxes Expense	M35		8 4 7 62		11
12			Social Security Tax Payable				3 7 9 44	12
13			Medicare Tax Payable				8 8 74	13
14			Unemployment Tax Payable—Federal				4 8 96	14
15			Unemployment Tax Payable—State				3 3 0 48	15
16								16
17								17
18								18
19								19
20								20
21								21
22								22
23								23
24								24
25								25

1., 2.

CASH PAYMENTS JOURNAL

PAGE 14

	DATE		ACCOUNT TITLE	CK. NO.	POST. REF.	GENERAL DEBIT (1)	GENERAL CREDIT (2)	ACCOUNTS PAYABLE DEBIT (3)	PURCHASES DISCOUNT CREDIT (4)	CASH CREDIT (5)	
1	Jan.	31	Salary Expense	555		5 9 2 0 00				5 1 0 7 12	1
2			Employee Income Tax Payable				3 6 0 00				2
3			Social Security Tax Payable				3 6 7 04				3
4			Medicare Tax Payable				8 5 84				4
5	Feb.	15	Employee Income Tax Payable	575		3 6 0 00				1 2 6 5 76	5
6			Social Security Tax Payable			7 3 4 08					6
7			Medicare Tax Payable			1 7 1 68					7
8		28	Salary Expense	601		6 0 5 8 00				5 2 2 2 56	8
9			Employee Income Tax Payable				3 7 2 00				9
10			Social Security Tax Payable				3 7 5 60				10
11			Medicare Tax Payable				8 7 84				11
12	Mar.	15	Employee Income Tax Payable	624		3 7 2 00				1 2 9 8 88	12
13			Social Security Tax Payable			7 5 1 20					13
14			Medicare Tax Payable			1 7 5 68					14
15		31	Salary Expense	658		6 1 2 0 00				5 2 5 7 82	15
16			Employee Income Tax Payable				3 9 4 00				16
17			Social Security Tax Payable				3 7 9 44				17
18			Medicare Tax Payable				8 8 74				18
19	Apr.	15	Employee Income Tax Payable	699		3 9 4 00				1 3 3 0 36	19
20			Social Security Tax Payable			7 5 8 88					20
21			Medicare Tax Payable			1 7 7 48					21
22		31	Unemployment Tax Payable—Federal	700		1 4 4 78				1 4 4 78	22
23		31	Unemployment Tax Payable—State	701		9 7 7 29				9 7 7 29	23
24		31	Totals			23 1 1 5 07	2 5 1 0 50			20 6 0 4 57	24

14-1 RECYCLING PROBLEM, p. D-11

Preparing an 8-column work sheet for a merchandising business

1., 2.

GENERAL JOURNAL

PAGE 12

DATE	ACCOUNT TITLE	DOC. NO.	POST. REF.	DEBIT	CREDIT	
20-- Dec. 15	Dividends	M114		7 5 0 0 00		1
	Dividends Payable				7 5 0 0 00	2
						3
						4
						5
						6
						7
						8

CASH PAYMENTS JOURNAL

PAGE 18

DATE	ACCOUNT TITLE	CK. NO.	POST. REF.	GENERAL DEBIT	GENERAL CREDIT	ACCOUNTS PAYABLE DEBIT	PURCHASES DISCOUNT CREDIT	CASH CREDIT	
20-- Jan. 15	Dividends Payable	924		7 5 0 0 00				7 5 0 0 00	1
									2
									3
									4
									5
									6
									7
									8

3., 4., 5.

Audio Source, Inc.

Work Sheet

For Year Ended December 31, 20 – –

ACCOUNT TITLE	TRIAL BALANCE		ADJUSTMENTS		INCOME STATEMENT		BALANCE SHEET	
	DEBIT	CREDIT	DEBIT	CREDIT	DEBIT	CREDIT	DEBIT	CREDIT
1 Cash	24 640 00						24 640 00	
2 Petty Cash	5 00 00						5 00 00	
3 Accounts Receivable	24 480 82						24 480 82	
4 Allow. for Uncoll. Accts.		1 48 33		(a) 2 480 00				2 628 33
5 Merchandise Inventory	267 980 00		(b) 2 481 36				270 461 36	
6 Supplies—Office	6 100 00			(c) 5 018 66			1 081 34	
7 Supplies—Store	6 500 00			(d) 4 914 10			1 585 90	
8 Prepaid Insurance	5 160 00			(e) 5 000 00			1 60 00	
9 Office Equipment	37 483 00						37 483 00	
10 Acc. Depr.—Office Equipment		22 489 00		(f) 6 140 00				28 629 00
11 Store Equipment	25 489 00						25 489 00	
12 Acc. Depr.—Store Equipment		16 493 00		(g) 5 520 00				22 013 00
13 Accounts Payable		11 665 00						11 665 00
14 Federal Income Tax Payable				(h) 1 318 66				1 318 66
15 Emp. Income Tax Payable		6 50 00						6 50 00
16 Social Security Tax Payable		7 57 76						7 57 76
17 Medicare Tax Payable		1 77 22						1 77 22
18 Sales Tax Payable		1 140 00						1 140 00
19 Unemployment Tax Pay.—Fed.		41 60						41 60
20 Unemployment Tax Pay.—State		2 80 80						2 80 80
21 Health Ins. Premiums Pay.		1 40 00						1 40 00
22 U.S. Savings Bonds Payable		60 00						60 00
23 United Way Donations Pay.		45 00						45 00
24 Dividends Payable		7 500 00						7 500 00
25 Capital Stock		100 000 00						100 000 00
26 Retained Earnings		99 977 67						99 977 67

Before Federal Income Tax:
Total of Income Statement Credit column $904,190.02
Total of Income Statement Debit column $704,013.98
Net Income before Federal Income Tax $200,176.04

14-1 RECYCLING PROBLEM (concluded)

Audio Source, Inc.

Work Sheet

For Year Ended December 31, 20 – –

	ACCOUNT TITLE	1 TRIAL BALANCE DEBIT	2 TRIAL BALANCE CREDIT	3 ADJUSTMENTS DEBIT	4 ADJUSTMENTS CREDIT	5 INCOME STATEMENT DEBIT	6 INCOME STATEMENT CREDIT	7 BALANCE SHEET DEBIT	8 BALANCE SHEET CREDIT	
27	Dividends	30 0 0 0 00						30 0 0 0 00		27
28	Income Summary				(b) 2 4 8 1 36		2 4 8 1 36			28
29	Sales		887 4 5 0 00				887 4 5 0 00			29
30	Sales Discount	5 1 1 8 36				5 1 1 8 36				30
31	Sales Returns and Allowances	7 1 8 4 69				7 1 8 4 69				31
32	Purchases	402 3 0 0 00				402 3 0 0 00				32
33	Purchases Discount		4 1 1 8 18				4 1 1 8 18			33
34	Purch. Returns and Allowances		10 1 4 0 48				10 1 4 0 48			34
35	Advertising Expense	5 6 8 0 00				5 6 8 0 00				35
36	Cash Short and Over	1 2 15				1 2 15				36
37	Credit Card Fee Expense	2 3 1 5 00				2 3 1 5 00				37
38	Depr. Exp.—Office Equipment			(f) 6 1 4 0 00		6 1 4 0 00				38
39	Depr. Exp.—Store Equipment			(g) 5 5 2 0 00		5 5 2 0 00				39
40	Insurance Expense			(e) 5 0 0 0 00		5 0 0 0 00				40
41	Miscellaneous Expense	2 8 3 0 00				2 8 3 0 00				41
42	Payroll Taxes Expense	27 8 5 1 58				27 8 5 1 58				42
43	Rent Expense	17 2 8 0 00				17 2 8 0 00				43
44	Salary Expense	201 0 9 4 44				201 0 9 4 44				44
45	Supplies Expense—Office			(c) 5 0 1 8 66		5 0 1 8 66				45
46	Supplies Expense—Store			(d) 4 9 1 4 10		4 9 1 4 10				46
47	Uncollectible Accts. Expense			(a) 2 4 8 0 00		2 4 8 0 00				47
48	Utilities Expense	3 2 7 5 00				3 2 7 5 00				48
49	Federal Income Tax Expense	60 0 0 0 00		(h) 1 3 1 8 66		61 3 1 8 66				49
50		1163 2 7 4 04	1163 2 7 4 04	32 8 7 2 78	32 8 7 2 78	765 3 3 2 64	904 1 9 0 02	415 8 8 1 42	277 0 2 4 04	50
51	*Net Inc. after Federal Inc. Tax*					138 8 5 7 38			138 8 5 7 38	51
52						904 1 9 0 02	904 1 9 0 02	415 8 8 1 42	415 8 8 1 42	52

Federal Income Tax:	Rate	Tax
First $50,000	15%	$ 7,500.00
Next $25,000	25%	$ 6,250.00
Next $25,000	34%	$ 8,500.00
$200,176.04 − $100,000.00 = *$100,176.04*	39%	$39,068.66
Total Federal Income Tax		$61,318.66

15-1 RECYCLING PROBLEM, p. D-11

Preparing financial statements

Hawkins Parts, Inc.

Work Sheet

For Year Ended December 31, 20 – –

	ACCOUNT TITLE	TRIAL BALANCE		ADJUSTMENTS		INCOME STATEMENT		BALANCE SHEET		
		DEBIT	CREDIT	DEBIT	CREDIT	DEBIT	CREDIT	DEBIT	CREDIT	
1	Cash	1415800						1415800		1
2	Petty Cash	25000						25000		2
3	Accounts Receivable	2218422						2218422		3
4	Allow. for Uncoll. Accts.		14833		(e) 265600				280433	4
5	Merchandise Inventory	23114825		(d) 481900				23596725		5
6	Supplies—Office	812500			(a) 695000			117500		6
7	Supplies—Store	481936			(b) 441811			40125		7
8	Prepaid Insurance	1280000			(c) 1200000			80000		8
9	Office Equipment	3314800						3314800		9
10	Acc. Depr.—Office Equipment		1844000		(f) 514800				2358800	10
11	Store Equipment	4218400						4218400		11
12	Acc. Depr.—Store Equipment		2299400		(g) 418400				2717800	12
13	Accounts Payable		2215400						2215400	13
14	Federal Income Tax Payable				(h) 1280772				1280772	14
15	Emp. Income Tax Payable		72000						72000	15
16	Social Security Tax Payable		64778						64778	16
17	Medicare Tax Payable		15150						15150	17
18	Sales Tax Payable		415400						415400	18
19	Unemployment Tax Pay.—Fed.		6400						6400	19
20	Unemployment Tax Pay.—State		43200						43200	20
21	Health Ins. Premiums Pay.		20000						20000	21
22	U.S. Savings Bonds Payable		8000						8000	22
23	United Way Donations Pay.		6000						6000	23
24	Dividends Payable		1000000						1000000	24
25	Capital Stock		32000000						32000000	25
26	Retained Earnings		11203995						11203995	26

Hawkins Parts, Inc.

Work Sheet

For Year Ended December 31, 20 – –

	ACCOUNT TITLE	TRIAL BALANCE DEBIT	TRIAL BALANCE CREDIT	ADJUSTMENTS DEBIT	ADJUSTMENTS CREDIT	INCOME STATEMENT DEBIT	INCOME STATEMENT CREDIT	BALANCE SHEET DEBIT	BALANCE SHEET CREDIT	
27	Dividends	40 000 00						40 000 00		27
28	Income Summary				(d) 4 819 00		4 819 00			28
29	Sales		928 148 06				928 148 06			29
30	Sales Discount	4 148 08				4 148 08				30
31	Sales Returns and Allowances	6 114 99				6 114 99				31
32	Purchases	414 810 09				414 810 09				32
33	Purchases Discount		3 184 07				3 184 07			33
34	Purch. Returns and Allowances		9 448 97				9 448 97			34
35	Advertising Expense	25 110 05				25 110 05				35
36	Cash Short and Over	2 505				2 505				36
37	Credit Card Fee Expense	6 480 02				6 480 02				37
38	Depr. Exp.—Office Equipment			(f) 5 148 00		5 148 00				38
39	Depr. Exp.—Store Equipment			(g) 4 184 00		4 184 00				39
40	Insurance Expense			(c) 12 000 00		12 000 00				40
41	Miscellaneous Expense	16 481 00				16 481 00				41
42	Payroll Taxes Expense	23 481 55				23 481 55				42
43	Rent Expense	16 000 00				16 000 00				43
44	Salary Expense	189 480 91				189 480 91				44
45	Supplies Expense—Office			(a) 6 950 00		6 950 00				45
46	Supplies Expense—Store			(b) 4 418 11		4 418 11				46
47	Uncollectible Accts. Expense			(e) 2 656 00		2 656 00				47
48	Utilities Expense	4 118 09				4 118 09				48
49	Federal Income Tax Expense	50 000 00		(h) 12 807 72		62 807 72				49
50		1165 066 66	1165 066 66	52 982 83	52 982 83	804 413 66	945 600 10	390 267 72	249 081 28	50
51	Net Inc. after Federal Inc. Tax					141 186 44			141 186 44	51
52						945 600 10	945 600 10	390 267 72	390 267 72	52

15-1   RECYCLING PROBLEM (continued)

1.

Hawkins Parts, Inc.

Income Statement

For Year Ended December 31, 20 – –

					% OF NET SALES
Operating Revenue:					
Net Sales			928 1 4 8 06		
Less: Sales Discount		4 1 4 8 08			
Sales Ret. and Allow.		6 1 1 4 99	10 2 6 3 07		
Net Sales				917 8 8 4 99	100.0
Cost of Merchandise Sold:					
Merchandise Inventory, Jan. 1, 20 – –			231 1 4 8 25		
Purchases		414 8 1 0 09			
Less: Purchases Discount	3 1 8 4 07				
Purch. Ret. and Allow.	9 4 4 8 97	12 6 3 3 04			
Net Purchases			402 1 7 7 05		
Total Cost of Mdse. Avail. for Sale			633 3 2 5 30		
Less Mdse. Inventory, Dec. 31, 20 – –			235 9 6 7 25		
Cost of Merchandise Sold				397 3 5 8 05	43.3
Gross Profit on Operations				520 5 2 6 94	56.7
Operating Expenses:					
Advertising Expense			25 1 1 0 05		
Cash Short and Over			2 5 05		
Credit Card Fee Expense			6 4 8 0 02		
Depr. Exp.—Office Equipment			5 1 4 8 00		
Depr. Exp.—Store Equipment			4 1 8 4 00		
Insurance Expense			12 0 0 0 00		
Miscellaneous Expense			16 4 8 1 00		
Payroll Taxes Expense			23 4 8 1 55		
Rent Expense			16 0 0 0 00		
Salary Expense			189 4 8 0 91		
Supplies Expense—Office			6 9 5 0 00		
Supplies Expense—Store			4 4 1 8 11		
Uncollectible Accounts Expense			2 6 5 6 00		
Utilities Expense			4 1 1 8 09		
Total Operating Expenses				316 5 3 2 78	34.5
Net Income before Income Tax				203 9 9 4 16	22.2
Less Federal Income Tax Expense				62 8 0 7 72	
Net Income after Federal Income Tax				141 1 8 6 44	

2.

Hawkins Parts, Inc.

Statement of Stockholders' Equity

For Year Ended December 31, 20--

Capital Stock:			
$1.00 per Share			
January 1, 20--, 30,000 Shares Issued		30 0 0 0 00	
Issued during Current Year, 2,000 Shares		2 0 0 0 00	
Balance, December 31, 20--, 32,000 Shares Issued			32 0 0 0 00
Retained Earnings:			
Balance, January 1, 20--		112 0 3 9 95	
Net Income after Federal Income Tax for 20--	141 1 8 6 44		
Less Dividends Declared during 20--	40 0 0 0 00		
Net Increase during 20--		101 1 8 6 44	
Balance, December 31, 20--			213 2 2 6 39
Total Stockholders' Equity, December 31, 20--			245 2 2 6 39

15-1   RECYCLING PROBLEM (continued)

3.

Hawkins Parts, Inc.

Balance Sheet

December 31, 20--

Assets			
Current Assets:			
Cash		14 1 5 8 00	
Petty Cash		2 5 0 00	
Accounts Receivable	22 1 8 4 22		
Less Allowance for Uncollectible Accounts	2 8 0 4 33	19 3 7 9 89	
Merchandise Inventory		235 9 6 7 25	
Supplies—Office		1 1 7 5 00	
Supplies—Store		4 0 1 25	
Prepaid Insurance		8 0 0 00	
Total Current Assets			272 1 3 1 39
Plant Assets:			
Office Equipment	33 1 4 8 00		
Less Accumulated Depreciation—Office Equipment	23 5 8 8 00	9 5 6 0 00	
Store Equipment	42 1 8 4 00		
Less Accumulated Depreciation—Store Equipment	27 1 7 8 00	15 0 0 6 00	
Total Plant Assets			24 5 6 6 00
Total Assets			296 6 9 7 39
Liabilities			
Current Liabilities:			
Accounts Payable		22 1 5 4 00	
Federal Income Tax Payable		12 8 0 7 72	
Employee Income Tax Payable		7 2 0 00	
Social Security Tax Payable		6 4 7 78	
Medicare Tax Payable		1 5 1 50	
Sales Tax Payable		4 1 5 4 00	
Unemployment Tax Payable—Federal		6 4 00	
Unemployment Tax Payable—State		4 3 2 00	
Health Insurance Premiums Payable		2 0 0 00	
U.S. Savings Bonds Payable		8 0 00	
United Way Donations Payable		6 0 00	
Dividends Payable		10 0 0 0 00	
Total Liabilities			51 4 7 1 00
Stockholders' Equity			
Capital Stock		32 0 0 0 00	
Retained Earnings		213 2 2 6 39	
Total Stockholders' Equity			245 2 2 6 39
Total Liabilities and Stockholders' Equity			296 6 9 7 39

4.

Earnings per Share

Net Income after Federal Income Tax	÷	Number of Shares Outstanding	=	Earnings per Share
$ 141,186.44	÷	32,000	=	$ 4.41

Price-Earnings Ratio

Market Price per Share	÷	Earnings per Share	=	Price-Earnings Ratio
$ 89.00	÷	$ 4.41	=	20.2

16-1 RECYCLING PROBLEM, p. D-12

Journalizing and posting adjusting and closing entries; preparing a post-closing trial balance

1.

GENERAL JOURNAL PAGE 18

	DATE		ACCOUNT TITLE	DOC. NO.	POST. REF.	DEBIT	CREDIT	
1			*Adjusting Entries*					1
2	Dec.	31	Uncollectible Accounts Expense	6160		2 2 1 5 00		2
3			Allowance for Uncoll. Accounts	1135			2 2 1 5 00	3
4		31	Merchandise Inventory	1140		4 8 1 9 00		4
5			Income Summary	3140			4 8 1 9 00	5
6		31	Supplies Expense—Office	6150		6 1 0 6 00		6
7			Supplies—Office	1145			6 1 0 6 00	7
8		31	Supplies Expense—Store	6155		3 1 5 4 00		8
9			Supplies—Store	1150			3 1 5 4 00	9
10		31	Insurance Expense	6125		9 6 0 0 00		10
11			Prepaid Insurance	1160			9 6 0 0 00	11
12		31	Depreciation Exp.—Office Equipment	6115		4 4 2 0 00		12
13			Accum. Depr.—Office Equipment	1210			4 4 2 0 00	13
14		31	Depreciation Exp.—Store Equipment	6120		4 9 5 0 00		14
15			Accum. Depr.—Store Equipment	1220			4 9 5 0 00	15
16		31	Federal Income Tax Expense	7105		6 4 2 9 62		16
17			Federal Income Tax Payable	2120			6 4 2 9 62	17
18								18
19								19
20								20
21								21
22								22
23								23
24								24
25								25
26								26
27								27
28								28
29								29
30								30
31								31
32								32

3.

GENERAL JOURNAL

PAGE 19

	DATE		ACCOUNT TITLE	DOC. NO.	POST. REF.	DEBIT	CREDIT	
1			*Closing Entries*					1
2	*Dec.* 20--	*31*	*Sales*		4110	742 5 1 8 45		2
3			*Purchases Discount*		5120	2 5 4 7 26		3
4			*Purchases Ret. and Allow.*		5130	7 5 5 9 18		4
5			*Income Summary*		3140		752 6 2 4 89	5
6		*31*	*Income Summary*		3140	641 8 7 4 48		6
7			*Sales Discount*		4120		3 3 1 8 46	7
8			*Sales Returns and Allow.*		4130		4 8 9 1 99	8
9			*Purchases*		5110		331 8 4 8 07	9
10			*Advertising Expense*		6105		20 0 8 8 04	10
11			*Cash Short and Over*		6107		2 0 04	11
12			*Credit Card Fee Expense*		6110		5 1 8 4 02	12
13			*Depr. Exp.—Office Equipment*		6115		4 4 2 0 00	13
14			*Depr. Exp.—Store Equipment*		6120		4 9 5 0 00	14
15			*Insurance Expense*		6125		9 6 0 0 00	15
16			*Miscellaneous Expense*		6130		13 1 8 4 80	16
17			*Payroll Taxes Expense*		6135		18 7 8 5 24	17
18			*Rent Expense*		6140		12 8 0 0 00	18
19			*Salary Expense*		6145		151 5 8 4 73	19
20			*Supplies Expense—Office*		6150		6 1 0 6 00	20
21			*Supplies Expense—Store*		6155		3 1 5 4 00	21
22			*Uncollectible Accounts Expense*		6160		2 2 1 5 00	22
23			*Utilities Expense*		6170		3 2 9 4 47	23
24			*Federal Income Tax Expense*		7105		46 4 2 9 62	24
25		*31*	*Income Summary*		3140	115 5 6 9 41		25
26			*Retained Earnings*		3120		115 5 6 9 41	26
27		*31*	*Retained Earnings*		3120	32 0 0 0 00		27
28			*Dividends*		3130		32 0 0 0 00	28
29								29
30								30
31								31
32								32
33								33

16-1 RECYCLING PROBLEM (continued)

2., 4., 5.   **GENERAL LEDGER**

ACCOUNT Cash   ACCOUNT NO. 1110

DATE		ITEM	POST. REF.	DEBIT	CREDIT	BALANCE DEBIT	BALANCE CREDIT
20-- Dec.	31	Balance	✔			11 3 2 6 40	

ACCOUNT Petty Cash   ACCOUNT NO. 1120

DATE		ITEM	POST. REF.	DEBIT	CREDIT	BALANCE DEBIT	BALANCE CREDIT
20-- Dec.	31	Balance	✔			2 0 0 00	

ACCOUNT Accounts Receivable   ACCOUNT NO. 1130

DATE		ITEM	POST. REF.	DEBIT	CREDIT	BALANCE DEBIT	BALANCE CREDIT
20-- Dec.	31	Balance	✔			17 7 4 7 38	

ACCOUNT Allow. for Uncoll. Accts.   ACCOUNT NO. 1135

DATE		ITEM	POST. REF.	DEBIT	CREDIT	BALANCE DEBIT	BALANCE CREDIT
20-- Dec.	31	Balance	✔				1 1 8 66
	31		G18		2 2 1 5 00		2 3 3 3 66

ACCOUNT Merchandise Inventory   ACCOUNT NO. 1140

DATE		ITEM	POST. REF.	DEBIT	CREDIT	BALANCE DEBIT	BALANCE CREDIT
20-- Dec.	31	Balance	✔			184 9 1 8 60	
	31		G18	4 8 1 9 00		189 7 3 7 60	

ACCOUNT Supplies—Office   ACCOUNT NO. 1145

DATE		ITEM	POST. REF.	DEBIT	CREDIT	BALANCE DEBIT	BALANCE CREDIT
20-- Dec.	31	Balance	✔			6 5 0 0 00	
	31		G18		6 1 0 6 00	3 9 4 00	

GENERAL LEDGER

ACCOUNT Supplies—Store   ACCOUNT NO. 1150

DATE	ITEM	POST. REF.	DEBIT	CREDIT	BALANCE DEBIT	BALANCE CREDIT
20-- Dec. 31	Balance	✔			3 855 49	
31		G18		3 154 00	701 49	

ACCOUNT Prepaid Insurance   ACCOUNT NO. 1160

DATE	ITEM	POST. REF.	DEBIT	CREDIT	BALANCE DEBIT	BALANCE CREDIT
20-- Dec. 31	Balance	✔			10 240 00	
31		G18		9 600 00	640 00	

ACCOUNT Office Equipment   ACCOUNT NO. 1205

DATE	ITEM	POST. REF.	DEBIT	CREDIT	BALANCE DEBIT	BALANCE CREDIT
20-- Dec. 31	Balance	✔			26 518 40	

ACCOUNT Acc. Depr.—Office Equipment   ACCOUNT NO. 1210

DATE	ITEM	POST. REF.	DEBIT	CREDIT	BALANCE DEBIT	BALANCE CREDIT
20-- Dec. 31	Balance	✔				14 752 00
31		G18		4 420 00		19 172 00

ACCOUNT Store Equipment   ACCOUNT NO. 1215

DATE	ITEM	POST. REF.	DEBIT	CREDIT	BALANCE DEBIT	BALANCE CREDIT
20-- Dec. 31	Balance	✔			33 747 20	

ACCOUNT Acc. Depr.—Store Equipment   ACCOUNT NO. 1220

DATE	ITEM	POST. REF.	DEBIT	CREDIT	BALANCE DEBIT	BALANCE CREDIT
20-- Dec. 31	Balance	✔				18 395 20
31		G18		4 950 00		23 345 20

16-1   RECYCLING PROBLEM (continued)

GENERAL LEDGER

ACCOUNT Accounts Payable   ACCOUNT NO. 2110

DATE	ITEM	POST. REF.	DEBIT	CREDIT	BALANCE DEBIT	BALANCE CREDIT
20-- Dec. 31	Balance	✔				17 7 2 3 20

ACCOUNT Federal Income Tax Payable   ACCOUNT NO. 2120

DATE	ITEM	POST. REF.	DEBIT	CREDIT	BALANCE DEBIT	BALANCE CREDIT
20-- Dec. 31		G18	6 4 2 9 62			6 4 2 9 62

ACCOUNT Employee Income Tax Payable   ACCOUNT NO. 2130

DATE	ITEM	POST. REF.	DEBIT	CREDIT	BALANCE DEBIT	BALANCE CREDIT
20-- Dec. 31	Balance	✔				5 7 6 00

ACCOUNT Social Security Tax Payable   ACCOUNT NO. 2135

DATE	ITEM	POST. REF.	DEBIT	CREDIT	BALANCE DEBIT	BALANCE CREDIT
20-- Dec. 31	Balance	✔				5 1 8 22

ACCOUNT Medicare Tax Payable   ACCOUNT NO. 2140

DATE	ITEM	POST. REF.	DEBIT	CREDIT	BALANCE DEBIT	BALANCE CREDIT
20-- Dec. 31	Balance	✔				1 2 1 20

ACCOUNT Sales Tax Payable   ACCOUNT NO. 2145

DATE	ITEM	POST. REF.	DEBIT	CREDIT	BALANCE DEBIT	BALANCE CREDIT
20-- Dec. 31	Balance	✔				3 3 2 3 20

ACCOUNT Unemployment Tax Payable—Federal   ACCOUNT NO. 2150

DATE	ITEM	POST. REF.	DEBIT	CREDIT	BALANCE DEBIT	BALANCE CREDIT
20-- Dec. 31	Balance	✔				5 1 20

GENERAL LEDGER

ACCOUNT **Unemployment Tax Payable—State**   ACCOUNT NO. **2155**

DATE	ITEM	POST. REF.	DEBIT	CREDIT	BALANCE DEBIT	BALANCE CREDIT
Dec. 31	Balance	✔				3 4 5 60

ACCOUNT **Health Insurance Premiums Payable**   ACCOUNT NO. **2160**

DATE	ITEM	POST. REF.	DEBIT	CREDIT	BALANCE DEBIT	BALANCE CREDIT
Dec. 31	Balance	✔				1 6 0 00

ACCOUNT **U.S. Savings Bonds Payable**   ACCOUNT NO. **2165**

DATE	ITEM	POST. REF.	DEBIT	CREDIT	BALANCE DEBIT	BALANCE CREDIT
Dec. 31	Balance	✔				6 4 00

ACCOUNT **United Way Donations Payable**   ACCOUNT NO. **2170**

DATE	ITEM	POST. REF.	DEBIT	CREDIT	BALANCE DEBIT	BALANCE CREDIT
Dec. 31	Balance	✔				4 8 00

ACCOUNT **Dividends Payable**   ACCOUNT NO. **2180**

DATE	ITEM	POST. REF.	DEBIT	CREDIT	BALANCE DEBIT	BALANCE CREDIT
Dec. 31	Balance	✔				8 0 0 0 00

ACCOUNT **Capital Stock**   ACCOUNT NO. **3110**

DATE	ITEM	POST. REF.	DEBIT	CREDIT	BALANCE DEBIT	BALANCE CREDIT
Dec. 31	Balance	✔				25 6 0 0 00

16-1 RECYCLING PROBLEM (continued)

GENERAL LEDGER

ACCOUNT **Retained Earnings** ACCOUNT NO. 3120

DATE		ITEM	POST. REF.	DEBIT	CREDIT	BALANCE DEBIT	BALANCE CREDIT
Dec.	1	Balance	✔				89 6 3 1 96
	31		G19		115 5 6 9 41		205 2 0 1 37
	31		G19	32 0 0 0 00			173 2 0 1 37

ACCOUNT **Dividends** ACCOUNT NO. 3130

DATE		ITEM	POST. REF.	DEBIT	CREDIT	BALANCE DEBIT	BALANCE CREDIT
Dec.	31	Balance	✔			32 0 0 0 00	
	31		G19		32 0 0 0 00	—	

ACCOUNT **Income Summary** ACCOUNT NO. 3140

DATE		ITEM	POST. REF.	DEBIT	CREDIT	BALANCE DEBIT	BALANCE CREDIT
Dec.	31		G18		4 8 1 9 00		4 8 1 9 00
	31		G19		752 6 2 4 89		757 4 4 3 89
	31		G19	641 8 7 4 48			115 5 6 9 41
	31		G19	115 5 6 9 41		—	—

ACCOUNT **Sales** ACCOUNT NO. 4110

DATE		ITEM	POST. REF.	DEBIT	CREDIT	BALANCE DEBIT	BALANCE CREDIT
Dec.	31	Balance	✔				742 5 1 8 45
	31		G19	742 5 1 8 45			—

ACCOUNT **Sales Discount** ACCOUNT NO. 4120

DATE		ITEM	POST. REF.	DEBIT	CREDIT	BALANCE DEBIT	BALANCE CREDIT
Dec.	31	Balance	✔			3 3 1 8 46	
	31		G19		3 3 1 8 46	—	

ACCOUNT **Sales Returns and Allowances** ACCOUNT NO. 4130

DATE		ITEM	POST. REF.	DEBIT	CREDIT	BALANCE DEBIT	BALANCE CREDIT
Dec.	31	Balance	✔			4 8 9 1 99	
	31		G19		4 8 9 1 99	—	

GENERAL LEDGER

ACCOUNT Purchases — ACCOUNT NO. 5110

DATE		ITEM	POST. REF.	DEBIT	CREDIT	BALANCE DEBIT	BALANCE CREDIT
Dec. 20--	31	Balance	✔			331 848 07	
	31		G19		331 848 07		

ACCOUNT Purchases Discount — ACCOUNT NO. 5120

DATE		ITEM	POST. REF.	DEBIT	CREDIT	BALANCE DEBIT	BALANCE CREDIT
Dec. 20--	31	Balance	✔				2 547 26
	31		G19	2 547 26			

ACCOUNT Purch. Returns and Allowances — ACCOUNT NO. 5130

DATE		ITEM	POST. REF.	DEBIT	CREDIT	BALANCE DEBIT	BALANCE CREDIT
Dec. 20--	31	Balance	✔				7 559 18
	31		G19	7 559 18			

ACCOUNT Advertising Expense — ACCOUNT NO. 6105

DATE		ITEM	POST. REF.	DEBIT	CREDIT	BALANCE DEBIT	BALANCE CREDIT
Dec. 20--	31	Balance	✔			20 088 04	
	31		G19		20 088 04		

ACCOUNT Cash Short and Over — ACCOUNT NO. 6107

DATE		ITEM	POST. REF.	DEBIT	CREDIT	BALANCE DEBIT	BALANCE CREDIT
Dec. 20--	31	Balance	✔			2 0 04	
	31		G19		2 0 04		

ACCOUNT Credit Card Fee Expense — ACCOUNT NO. 6110

DATE		ITEM	POST. REF.	DEBIT	CREDIT	BALANCE DEBIT	BALANCE CREDIT
Dec. 20--	31	Balance	✔			5 184 02	
	31		G19		5 184 02		

16-1   RECYCLING PROBLEM (continued)

GENERAL LEDGER

ACCOUNT Depr. Exp.—Office Equipment   ACCOUNT NO. 6115

DATE	ITEM	POST. REF.	DEBIT	CREDIT	BALANCE DEBIT	BALANCE CREDIT
20-- Dec. 31		G18	4 4 2 0 00		4 4 2 0 00	
31		G19		4 4 2 0 00		

ACCOUNT Depr. Exp.—Store Equipment   ACCOUNT NO. 6120

DATE	ITEM	POST. REF.	DEBIT	CREDIT	BALANCE DEBIT	BALANCE CREDIT
20-- Dec. 31		G18	4 9 5 0 00		4 9 5 0 00	
31		G19		4 9 5 0 00		

ACCOUNT Insurance Expense   ACCOUNT NO. 6125

DATE	ITEM	POST. REF.	DEBIT	CREDIT	BALANCE DEBIT	BALANCE CREDIT
20-- Dec. 31		G18	9 6 0 0 00		9 6 0 0 00	
31		G19		9 6 0 0 00		

ACCOUNT Miscellaneous Expense   ACCOUNT NO. 6130

DATE	ITEM	POST. REF.	DEBIT	CREDIT	BALANCE DEBIT	BALANCE CREDIT
20-- Dec. 31	Balance	✔			13 1 8 4 80	
31		G19		13 1 8 4 80		

ACCOUNT Payroll Taxes Expense   ACCOUNT NO. 6135

DATE	ITEM	POST. REF.	DEBIT	CREDIT	BALANCE DEBIT	BALANCE CREDIT
20-- Dec. 31	Balance	✔			18 7 8 5 24	
31		G19		18 7 8 5 24		

ACCOUNT Rent Expense   ACCOUNT NO. 6140

DATE	ITEM	POST. REF.	DEBIT	CREDIT	BALANCE DEBIT	BALANCE CREDIT
20-- Dec. 31	Balance	✔			12 8 0 0 00	
31		G19		12 8 0 0 00		

GENERAL LEDGER

ACCOUNT Salary Expense   ACCOUNT NO. 6145

DATE		ITEM	POST. REF.	DEBIT	CREDIT	BALANCE DEBIT	BALANCE CREDIT
Dec.	31	Balance	✔			151 584 73	
	31		G19		151 584 73	—	—

ACCOUNT Supplies Expense—Office   ACCOUNT NO. 6150

DATE		ITEM	POST. REF.	DEBIT	CREDIT	BALANCE DEBIT	BALANCE CREDIT
Dec.	31		G18	6 106 00		6 106 00	
	31		G19		6 106 00	—	

ACCOUNT Supplies Expense—Store   ACCOUNT NO. 6155

DATE		ITEM	POST. REF.	DEBIT	CREDIT	BALANCE DEBIT	BALANCE CREDIT
Dec.	31		G18	3 154 00		3 154 00	
	31		G19		3 154 00	—	

ACCOUNT Uncollectible Accounts Expense   ACCOUNT NO. 6160

DATE		ITEM	POST. REF.	DEBIT	CREDIT	BALANCE DEBIT	BALANCE CREDIT
Dec.	31		G18	2 215 00		2 215 00	
	31		G19		2 215 00	—	

ACCOUNT Utilities Expense   ACCOUNT NO. 6170

DATE		ITEM	POST. REF.	DEBIT	CREDIT	BALANCE DEBIT	BALANCE CREDIT
Dec.	31	Balance	✔			3 294 47	
	31		G19		3 294 47	—	

ACCOUNT Federal Income Tax Expense   ACCOUNT NO. 7105

DATE		ITEM	POST. REF.	DEBIT	CREDIT	BALANCE DEBIT	BALANCE CREDIT
Dec.	31	Balance	✔			40 000 00	
	31		G18	6 429 62		46 429 62	
	31		G19		46 429 62	—	

16-1 RECYCLING PROBLEM (concluded)

5.

Southern Fixtures, Inc.

Post-Closing Trial Balance

December 31, 20 – –

ACCOUNT TITLE	DEBIT	CREDIT
Cash	11 3 2 6 40	
Petty Cash	2 0 0 00	
Accounts Receivable	17 7 4 7 38	
Allow. for Uncoll. Accts.		2 3 3 3 66
Merchandise Inventory	189 7 3 7 60	
Supplies—Office	3 9 4 00	
Supplies—Store	7 0 1 49	
Prepaid Insurance	6 4 0 00	
Office Equipment	26 5 1 8 40	
Acc. Depr.—Office Equipment		19 1 7 2 00
Store Equipment	33 7 4 7 20	
Acc. Depr.—Store Equipment		23 3 4 5 20
Accounts Payable		17 7 2 3 20
Federal Income Tax Payable		6 4 2 9 62
Employee Income Tax Payable		5 7 6 00
Social Security Tax Payable		5 1 8 22
Medicare Tax Payable		1 2 1 20
Sales Tax Payable		3 3 2 3 20
Unemployment Tax Payable—Federal		5 1 20
Unemployment Tax Payable—State		3 4 5 60
Health Insurance Premiums Payable		1 6 0 00
U.S. Savings Bonds Payable		6 4 00
United Way Donations Payable		4 8 00
Dividends Payable		8 0 0 0 00
Capital Stock		25 6 0 0 00
Retained Earnings		173 2 0 1 37
Totals	281 0 1 2 47	281 0 1 2 47

17-1 RECYCLING PROBLEM, p. D-13

Recording entries for uncollectible accounts

1.

GENERAL JOURNAL — PAGE 10

	DATE		ACCOUNT TITLE	DOC. NO.	POST. REF.	DEBIT	CREDIT	
1	Oct.	6	Allowance for Uncollectible Accounts	M216	1130	2 8 4 75		1
2			Accounts Receivable/Chittenden Corp.		1125/120		2 8 4 75	2
3		19	Allowance for Uncollectible Accounts	M221	1130	5 7 4 10		3
4			Accounts Receivable/Foster Corp.		1125/140		5 7 4 10	4

2.

GENERAL JOURNAL — PAGE 11

	DATE		ACCOUNT TITLE	DOC. NO.	POST. REF.	DEBIT	CREDIT	
1	Nov.	5	Allowance for Uncollectible Accounts	M236	1130	8 0 4 24		1
2			Accounts Receivable/Agnew Company		1125/110		8 0 4 24	2
3		12	Accounts Receivable/Chittenden Corp.	M241	1125/120	2 8 4 75		3
4			Allowance for Uncollectible Accounts		1130		2 8 4 75	4
5		17	Accounts Receivable/Dionne, Inc.	M243	1125/130	4 6 8 30		5
6			Allowance for Uncollectible Accounts		1130		4 6 8 30	6

3.

GENERAL JOURNAL — PAGE 12

	DATE		ACCOUNT TITLE	DOC. NO.	POST. REF.	DEBIT	CREDIT	
1	Dec.	4	Allowance for Uncollectible Accounts	M257	1130	7 0 5 18		1
2			Accounts Receivable/Grant Company		1125/150		7 0 5 18	2
3		10	Accounts Receivable/Agnew Company	M259	1125/110	8 0 4 24		3
4			Allowance for Uncollectible Accounts		1130		8 0 4 24	4
5		21	Accounts Receivable/Foster Corp.	M265	1125/140	5 7 4 10		5
6			Allowance for Uncollectible Accounts		1130		5 7 4 10	6

4.

GENERAL JOURNAL — PAGE 13

	DATE		ACCOUNT TITLE	DOC. NO.	POST. REF.	DEBIT	CREDIT	
1			*Adjusting Entries*					1
2	Dec.	31	Uncollectible Accounts Expense		6165	11 8 5 1 92		2
3			Allowance for Uncollectible Accounts		1130		11 8 5 1 92	3

2.

CASH RECEIPTS JOURNAL

PAGE 11

	DATE	ACCOUNT TITLE	DOC. NO.	POST. REF.	GENERAL DEBIT	GENERAL CREDIT	ACCOUNTS RECEIVABLE CREDIT	SALES CREDIT	SALES TAX PAYABLE CREDIT	SALES DISCOUNT DEBIT	CASH DEBIT	
1	Nov. 12	Chittenden Corp.	R616	120			2 8 4 75				2 8 4 75	1
2	17	Dionne, Inc.	R627	130			4 6 8 30				4 6 8 30	2
3	30	Totals					7 5 3 05				7 5 3 05	3
4							(1125)				(1105)	4
5												5
6												6
7												7
8												8
9												9
10												10

3.

CASH RECEIPTS JOURNAL

PAGE 12

	DATE	ACCOUNT TITLE	DOC. NO.	POST. REF.	GENERAL DEBIT	GENERAL CREDIT	ACCOUNTS RECEIVABLE CREDIT	SALES CREDIT	SALES TAX PAYABLE CREDIT	SALES DISCOUNT DEBIT	CASH DEBIT	
1	Dec. 10	Agnew Company	R702	110			8 0 4 24				8 0 4 24	1
2	21	Foster Corp.	R729	140			5 7 4 10				5 7 4 10	2
3	31	Totals					1 3 7 8 34				1 3 7 8 34	3
4							(1125)				(1105)	4
5												5
6												6
7												7
8												8
9												9

17-1 RECYCLING PROBLEM (continued)

1., 2., 3., 4.   **GENERAL LEDGER**

ACCOUNT Cash   ACCOUNT NO. 1105

DATE		ITEM	POST. REF.	DEBIT	CREDIT	BALANCE DEBIT	BALANCE CREDIT
Oct.	1	Balance	✔			4 9 7 8 00	
Nov.	30		CR11	7 5 3 05		5 7 3 1 05	
Dec.	31		CR12	1 3 7 8 34		7 1 0 9 39	

ACCOUNT Accounts Receivable   ACCOUNT NO. 1125

DATE		ITEM	POST. REF.	DEBIT	CREDIT	BALANCE DEBIT	BALANCE CREDIT
Oct.	1	Balance	✔			62 4 8 6 25	
	6		G10		2 8 4 75	62 2 0 1 50	
	19		G10		5 7 4 10	61 6 2 7 40	
Nov.	5		G11		8 0 4 24	60 8 2 3 16	
	12		G11	2 8 4 75		61 1 0 7 91	
	17		G11	4 6 8 30		61 5 7 6 21	
	30		CR11		7 5 3 05	60 8 2 3 16	
Dec.	4		G12		7 0 5 18	60 1 1 7 98	
	10		G12	8 0 4 24		60 9 2 2 22	
	21		G12	5 7 4 10		61 4 9 6 32	
	31		CR12		1 3 7 8 34	60 1 1 7 98	

ACCOUNT Allowance for Uncollectible Accounts   ACCOUNT NO. 1130

DATE		ITEM	POST. REF.	DEBIT	CREDIT	BALANCE DEBIT	BALANCE CREDIT
Oct.	1	Balance	✔				2 4 1 8 19
	6		G10	2 8 4 75			2 1 3 3 44
	19		G10	5 7 4 10			1 5 5 9 34
Nov.	5		G11	8 0 4 24			7 5 5 10
	12		G11		2 8 4 75		1 0 3 9 85
	17		G11		4 6 8 30		1 5 0 8 15
Dec.	4		G12	7 0 5 18			8 0 2 97
	10		G12		8 0 4 24		1 6 0 7 21
	21		G12		5 7 4 10		2 1 8 1 31
	31		G13		11 8 5 1 92		14 0 3 3 23

ACCOUNT Uncollectible Accounts Expense   ACCOUNT NO. 6165

DATE		ITEM	POST. REF.	DEBIT	CREDIT	BALANCE DEBIT	BALANCE CREDIT
Dec.	31		G13	11 8 5 1 92		11 8 5 1 92	

1., 2., 3.   **ACCOUNTS RECEIVABLE LEDGER**

CUSTOMER Agnew Company   CUSTOMER NO. 110

DATE		ITEM	POST. REF.	DEBIT	CREDIT	DEBIT BALANCE
20-- June	7		S6	8 0 4 24		8 0 4 24
Nov.	5	*Written off*	G11		8 0 4 24	—
Dec.	10	*Reopen account*	G12	8 0 4 24		8 0 4 24
	10		CR12		8 0 4 24	—

CUSTOMER Chittenden Corp.   CUSTOMER NO. 120

DATE		ITEM	POST. REF.	DEBIT	CREDIT	DEBIT BALANCE
20-- May	13		S5	2 8 4 75		2 8 4 75
Oct.	6	*Written off*	G10		2 8 4 75	—
Nov.	12	*Reopen account*	G11	2 8 4 75		2 8 4 75
	12		CR11		2 8 4 75	—

CUSTOMER Dionne, Inc.   CUSTOMER NO. 130

DATE		ITEM	POST. REF.	DEBIT	CREDIT	DEBIT BALANCE
20-- Jan.	1	Balance	✔			4 6 8 30
Mar.	3	Written off	G3		4 6 8 30	—
Nov.	17	*Reopen account*	G11	4 6 8 30		4 6 8 30
	17		CR11		4 6 8 30	—

CUSTOMER Foster Corp.   CUSTOMER NO. 140

DATE		ITEM	POST. REF.	DEBIT	CREDIT	DEBIT BALANCE
20-- June	21		S6	5 7 4 10		5 7 4 10
Oct.	19	*Written off*	G10		5 7 4 10	—
Dec.	21	*Reopen account*	G12	5 7 4 10		5 7 4 10
	21		CR12		5 7 4 10	—

CUSTOMER Grant Company   CUSTOMER NO. 150

DATE		ITEM	POST. REF.	DEBIT	CREDIT	DEBIT BALANCE
20-- Jan.	1	Balance	✔			7 0 5 18
Dec.	4	*Written off*	G12		7 0 5 18	—

Recording transactions for plant assets

1.

CASH PAYMENTS JOURNAL

PAGE 1

	DATE	ACCOUNT TITLE	CK. NO.	POST. REF.	GENERAL DEBIT	GENERAL CREDIT	ACCOUNTS PAYABLE DEBIT	PURCHASES DISCOUNT CREDIT	CASH CREDIT	
					1	2	3	4	5	
1	20X1 Jan. 3	Office Equipment	168		90000				90000	1
2	Feb. 26	Property Tax Expense	216		868000				868000	2
3	Apr. 3	Store Equipment	275		300000				300000	3
4										4
5										5
6										6
7										7
8										8
9										9

5.

CASH RECEIPTS JOURNAL

PAGE 2

	DATE	ACCOUNT TITLE	DOC. NO.	POST. REF.	GENERAL DEBIT	GENERAL CREDIT	ACCOUNTS RECEIVABLE CREDIT	SALES CREDIT	SALES TAX PAYABLE CREDIT	SALES DISCOUNT DEBIT	CASH DEBIT	
					1	2	3	4	5	6	7	
1	20X5 Jan. 3	Accum. Depr.—Office Equip.	R7		80000						6000	1
2		Loss on Plant Assets			4000							2
3		Office Equipment				90000						3
4	June 29	Accum. Depr.—Store Equip.	R171		212500						95000	4
5		Store Equipment				300000						5
6		Gain on Plant Assets				7500						6
7												7
8												8
9												9

2., 4., 6.

<table>
<tr><td colspan="3">PLANT ASSET RECORD No. <u>642</u></td><td colspan="2">General Ledger Account No. <u>1205</u></td></tr>
<tr><td colspan="3">Description <u>Color Printer</u></td><td colspan="2">General Ledger Account <u>Office Equipment</u></td></tr>
</table>

PLANT ASSET RECORD No. <u>642</u>　　　General Ledger Account No. <u>1205</u>

Description <u>Color Printer</u>　　　General Ledger Account <u>Office Equipment</u>

Date Bought <u>January 3, 20X1</u>　　Serial Number <u>ZE532N34</u>　　Original Cost <u>$900.00</u>

Estimated Useful Life <u>4 years</u>　　Estimated Salvage Value <u>$100.00</u>　　Depreciation Method <u>Declining-balance</u>

Disposed of:　Discarded ______　Sold <u>✔</u>　Traded ______

Date <u>January 3, 20X5</u>　　Disposal Amount <u>$60.00</u>

YEAR	ANNUAL DEPRECIATION EXPENSE	ACCUMULATED DEPRECIATION	ENDING BOOK VALUE
20X1	$450.00	$450.00	$450.00
20X2	225.00	675.00	225.00
20X3	112.50	787.50	112.50
20X4	12.50	800.00	100.00

Continue record on back of card

3.

Plant asset: <u>Color Printer</u>　　Original cost: <u>$900.00</u>

Depreciation method: <u>Declining-balance</u>　　Estimated salvage value: <u>$100.00</u>

Estimated useful life: <u>4 years</u>

Year	Beginning Book Value	Declining-Balance Rate	Annual Depreciation	Ending Book Value
20X1	$900.00	50%	$450.00	$450.00
20X2	450.00	50%	225.00	225.00
20X3	225.00	50%	112.50	112.50
20X4	112.50	—	12.50	100.00

　　

18-1   RECYCLING PROBLEM (continued)

2., 4., 6.

PLANT ASSET RECORD No. **643**   General Ledger Account No. **1215**

Description **Store Display**   General Ledger Account **Store Equipment**

Date Bought **April 3, 20X1**   Serial Number **754NFE**   Original Cost **$3,000.00**

Estimated Useful Life **5 years**   Estimated Salvage Value **$500.00**   Depreciation Method **Straight-line**

Disposed of: Discarded __________   Sold **✔**   Traded __________

Date **June 29, 20X5**   Disposal Amount **$950.00**

YEAR	ANNUAL DEPRECIATION EXPENSE	ACCUMULATED DEPRECIATION	ENDING BOOK VALUE
20X1	$375.00	$ 375.00	$2,625.00
20X2	500.00	875.00	2,125.00
20X3	500.00	1,375.00	1,625.00
20X4	500.00	1,875.00	1,125.00
20X5	250.00	2,125.00	875.00

Continue record on back of card

3.

Plant asset: **Store Display**   Original cost: **$3,000.00**

Depreciation method: **Straight-line**   Estimated salvage value: **$500.00**

Estimated useful life: **5 years**

Year	Beginning Book Value	Annual Depreciation	Accumulated Depreciation	Ending Book Value
20X1	$3,000.00	$375.00	$ 375.00	$2,625.00
20X2	2,625.00	500.00	875.00	2,125.00
20X3	2,125.00	500.00	1,375.00	1,625.00
20X4	1,625.00	500.00	1,875.00	1,125.00
20X5	1,125.00	500.00	2,375.00	625.00
20X6	625.00	125.00	2,500.00	500.00

5.

GENERAL JOURNAL

PAGE 2

	DATE		ACCOUNT TITLE	DOC. NO.	POST. REF.	DEBIT	CREDIT	
1	*20X5* *June*	29	*Depreciation Expense—Store Equipment*	*M69*		2 5 0 00		1
2			*Accumulated Depreciation—Store Equipment*				2 5 0 00	2
3			*Adjusting Entries*					3
4	*Dec.*	31	*Depreciation Expense—Store Equipment*			17 7 6 5 00		4
5			*Accumulated Depreciation—Store Equipment*				17 7 6 5 00	5
6								6
7								7
8								8
9								9
10								10
11								11
12								12
13								13
14								14
15								15
16								16
17								17
18								18
19								19
20								20
21								21
22								22
23								23
24								24
25								25
26								26
27								27
28								28
29								29
30								30
31								31
32								32
33								33

19-1 RECYCLING PROBLEM, p. D-14

Determining the cost of inventory using the fifo, lifo, and weighted-average inventory costing methods

1.

FIFO Method

Purchase Dates	Units Purchased	Unit Price	Total Cost	FIFO Units on Hand	FIFO Cost
January 1, beginning inventory	3	$12.30	$ 36.90		
January 3, purchases	20	13.00	260.00		
March 29, purchases	20	13.20	264.00	2	$ 26.40
August 15, purchases	15	13.25	198.75	15	198.75
November 13, purchases	15	13.45	201.75	15	201.75
Totals	73		$961.40	32	$426.90

LIFO Method

Purchase Dates	Units Purchased	Unit Price	Total Cost	LIFO Units on Hand	LIFO Cost
January 1, beginning inventory	3	$12.30	$ 36.90	3	$ 36.90
January 3, purchases	20	13.00	260.00	20	260.00
March 29, purchases	20	13.20	264.00	9	118.80
August 15, purchases	15	13.25	198.75		
November 13, purchases	15	13.45	201.75		
Totals	73		$961.40	32	$415.70

Weighted-Average Method

Date	Purchases Units	Purchases Unit Price	Total Cost
January 1, beginning inventory	3	$12.30	$ 36.90
January 3, purchases	20	13.00	260.00
March 29, purchases	20	13.20	264.00
August 15, purchases	15	13.25	198.75
November 13, purchases	15	13.45	201.75
Totals	73		$961.40

Total of Beginning Inventory and Purchases	÷	Total Units	=	Weighted-Average Price per Unit
$961.40		73		$13.17

Units in Ending Inventory	×	Weighted-Average Price per Unit	=	Cost of Ending Inventory
32		$13.17		$421.44

2.

	Fifo	Lifo	Weighted-Average
Merchandise Available for Sale	*$961.40*	*$961.40*	*$961.40*
Ending Inventory	*426.90*	*415.70*	*421.44*
Cost of Merchandise Sold	*$534.50*	*$545.70*	*$539.96*

Highest Cost of Merchandise Sold: *lifo*

20-1   RECYCLING PROBLEM, pp. D-14, D-15

Journalizing notes payable and notes receivable transactions

1.

GENERAL JOURNAL   PAGE 3

	DATE		ACCOUNT TITLE	DOC. NO.	POST. REF.	DEBIT	CREDIT	
1	20-- Apr.	9	Notes Receivable	NR18		6 5 0 00		1
2			Accounts Receivable/Phillip Majure				6 5 0 00	2
3		16	Notes Receivable	NR19		2 4 5 0 00		3
4			Accounts Receivable/Avery Harris				2 4 5 0 00	4
5		20	Accounts Payable/Rossman Supply	M49		2 5 0 0 00		5
6			Notes Payable				2 5 0 0 00	6
7		22	Accounts Receivable/Patrick Isamen	M53		3 1 1 2 50		7
8			Notes Receivable				3 0 0 0 00	8
9			Interest Income				1 1 2 50	9
10								10

1.

CASH RECEIPTS JOURNAL   PAGE 6

	DATE		ACCOUNT TITLE	DOC. NO.	POST. REF.	GENERAL DEBIT	GENERAL CREDIT	ACCOUNTS RECEIVABLE CREDIT	SALES CREDIT	SALES TAX PAYABLE CREDIT	SALES DISCOUNT DEBIT	CASH DEBIT	
						1	2	3	4	5	6	7	
1	20-- Apr.	5	Notes Payable	R34			30 0 0 0 00					30 0 0 0 00	1
2		12	Notes Receivable	R67			9 0 0 00					9 2 7 00	2
3			Interest Income				2 7 00						3
4		19	Notes Receivable	R74			5 0 0 00					5 1 5 00	4
5			Interest Income				1 5 00						5
6		27	Notes Payable	R84			20 0 0 0 00					20 0 0 0 00	6
7		29	Notes Receivable	R89			1 8 0 0 00					1 8 8 1 00	7
8			Interest Income				8 1 00						8

2.

Calculations:

April 5, 90-Day Note

Maturity Date:		*Maturity Value:*
April 5–30	*25 days*	$30,000.00 × 10% × 90/360 = $750.00
May	*31 days*	$30,000.00 + $750.00 = $30,750.00
June	*30 days*	
July 1–4	*4 days*	
Total	*90 days*	

April 20, 90-Day Note

Maturity Date:		*Maturity Value:*
April 20–30	*10 days*	$2,500.00 × 15% × 90/360 = $93.75
May	*31 days*	$2,500.00 + $93.75 = $2,593.75
June	*30 days*	
July 1–19	*19 days*	
Total	*90 days*	

April 27, 120-Day Note

Maturity Date:		*Maturity Value:*
April 27–30	*3 days*	$20,000.00 × 12% × 120/360 = $800.00
May	*31 days*	$20,000.00 + $800.00 = $20,800.00
June	*30 days*	
July	*31 days*	
August 1–25	*25 days*	
Total	*120 days*	

20-1 RECYCLING PROBLEM (concluded)

3.

CASH PAYMENTS JOURNAL

PAGE 10

	DATE		ACCOUNT TITLE	CK. NO.	POST. REF.	GENERAL DEBIT	GENERAL CREDIT	ACCOUNTS PAYABLE DEBIT	PURCHASES DISCOUNT CREDIT	CASH CREDIT	
1	20-- July	4	Notes Payable	452		30 00 0 00				30 75 0 00	1
2			Interest Expense			7 5 0 00					2
3		19	Notes Payable	489		2 5 0 0 00				2 5 9 3 75	3
4			Interest Expense			9 3 75					4
5	Aug.	25	Notes Payable	672		20 00 0 00				20 80 0 00	5
6			Interest Expense			8 0 0 00					6
7											7
8											8
9											9
10											10
11											11
12											12
13											13
14											14
15											15
16											16
17											17
18											18
19											19
20											20
21											21
22											22
23											23

21-1   RECYCLING PROBLEM, p. D-15

Journalizing and posting entries for accrued interest revenue and expense

1.

Farrell Company

Work Sheet

For Year Ended December 31, 20X1

	ACCOUNT TITLE	TRIAL BALANCE		ADJUSTMENTS	
		DEBIT	CREDIT	DEBIT	CREDIT
4	Interest Receivable			(a) 20 80	
15	Interest Payable				(h) 27 20
50	Interest Income		1 897 00		(a) 20 80
51	Interest Expense	2 458 00		(h) 27 20	

NR18: $800 × .18 × 52/360 = $20.80 interest receivable on Dec. 31
NP: $4,800 × .12 × 17/360 = $27.20 interest payable on Dec. 31

2., 3.

GENERAL JOURNAL   PAGE 15

	DATE		ACCOUNT TITLE	DOC. NO.	POST. REF.	DEBIT	CREDIT	
1			*Adjusting Entries*					1
2	20X1 Dec.	31	Interest Receivable		1120	20 80		2
3			Interest Income		7110		20 80	3
4		31	Interest Expense		8105	27 20		4
5			Interest Payable		2110		27 20	5
6								6
7			*Closing Entries*					7
8	20X1 Dec.	31	Interest Income		7110	1 917 80		8
9			Income Summary		3120		1 917 80	9
10		31	Income Summary		3120	2 485 20		10
11			Interest Expense		8105		2 485 20	11

4.

GENERAL JOURNAL   PAGE 16

	DATE		ACCOUNT TITLE	DOC. NO.	POST. REF.	DEBIT	CREDIT	
1			*Reversing Entries*					1
2	20X2 Jan.	1	Interest Income		7110	20 80		2
3			Interest Receivable		1120		20 80	3
4		1	Interest Payable		2110	27 20		4
5			Interest Expense		8105		27 20	5

2., 3., 4., 5., 6.   **GENERAL LEDGER**

ACCOUNT Notes Receivable   ACCOUNT NO. 1115

DATE	ITEM	POST. REF.	DEBIT	CREDIT	BALANCE DEBIT	BALANCE CREDIT
Nov. 9		G14	8 0 0 00		8 0 0 00	
20X2 Feb. 7		CR13		8 0 0 00	—	—

ACCOUNT Interest Receivable   ACCOUNT NO. 1120

DATE	ITEM	POST. REF.	DEBIT	CREDIT	BALANCE DEBIT	BALANCE CREDIT
20X1 Dec. 31		G15	2 0 80		2 0 80	
20X2 Jan. 1		G16		2 0 80	—	—

ACCOUNT Notes Payable   ACCOUNT NO. 2105

DATE	ITEM	POST. REF.	DEBIT	CREDIT	BALANCE DEBIT	BALANCE CREDIT
Dec. 14		CR12		4 8 0 0 00		4 8 0 0 00
20X2 Apr. 13		CP18	4 8 0 0 00		—	—

ACCOUNT Interest Payable   ACCOUNT NO. 2110

DATE	ITEM	POST. REF.	DEBIT	CREDIT	BALANCE DEBIT	BALANCE CREDIT
20X1 Dec. 31		G15		2 7 20		2 7 20
20X2 Jan. 1		G16	2 7 20		—	—

21-1 RECYCLING PROBLEM (continued)

2., 3., 4., 5., 6.   GENERAL LEDGER

ACCOUNT Income Summary   ACCOUNT NO. 3120

DATE		ITEM	POST. REF.	DEBIT	CREDIT	BALANCE DEBIT	BALANCE CREDIT
20X1 Dec.	31		G15		1 9 1 7 80		1 9 1 7 80
	31		G15	2 4 8 5 20		5 6 7 40	

ACCOUNT Interest Income   ACCOUNT NO. 7110

DATE		ITEM	POST. REF.	DEBIT	CREDIT	BALANCE DEBIT	BALANCE CREDIT
Dec.	31		CR12		8 5 00		1 8 9 7 00
	31		G15		2 0 80		1 9 1 7 80
	31		G15	1 9 1 7 80		—	—
20X2 Jan.	1		G16		2 0 80		2 0 80
Feb.	7		CR13		3 6 00		1 5 20

ACCOUNT Interest Expense   ACCOUNT NO. 8105

DATE		ITEM	POST. REF.	DEBIT	CREDIT	BALANCE DEBIT	BALANCE CREDIT
Dec.	31		CP12	1 0 0 00		2 4 5 8 00	
	31		G15	2 7 20		2 4 8 5 20	
	31		G15		2 4 8 5 20	—	—
20X2 Jan.	1		G16		2 7 20		2 7 20
Apr.	13		CP18	1 9 2 00		1 6 4 80	

RECYCLING PROBLEM (concluded)

5.

CASH RECEIPTS JOURNAL

PAGE 13

	DATE		ACCOUNT TITLE	DOC. NO.	POST. REF.	GENERAL DEBIT	GENERAL CREDIT	ACCOUNTS RECEIVABLE CREDIT	SALES CREDIT	SALES TAX PAYABLE CREDIT	SALES DISCOUNT DEBIT	CASH DEBIT	
						1	2	3	4	5	6	7	
1	20X2 Feb.	7	Notes Receivable	R132	1115		8 0 0 00					8 3 6 00	1
2			Interest Income		7110		3 6 00						2
3													3
4													4
5													5
6													6
7													7
8													8
9													9
10													10

6.

CASH PAYMENTS JOURNAL

PAGE 18

	DATE		ACCOUNT TITLE	CK. NO.	POST. REF.	GENERAL DEBIT	GENERAL CREDIT	ACCOUNTS PAYABLE DEBIT	PURCHASES DISCOUNT CREDIT	CASH CREDIT	
						1	2	3	4	5	
1	20X2 Apr.	13	Notes Payable	342	2105	4 8 0 0 00				4 9 9 2 00	1
2			Interest Expense		8105	1 9 2 00					2
3											3
4											4
5											5
6											6
7											7
8											8
9											9

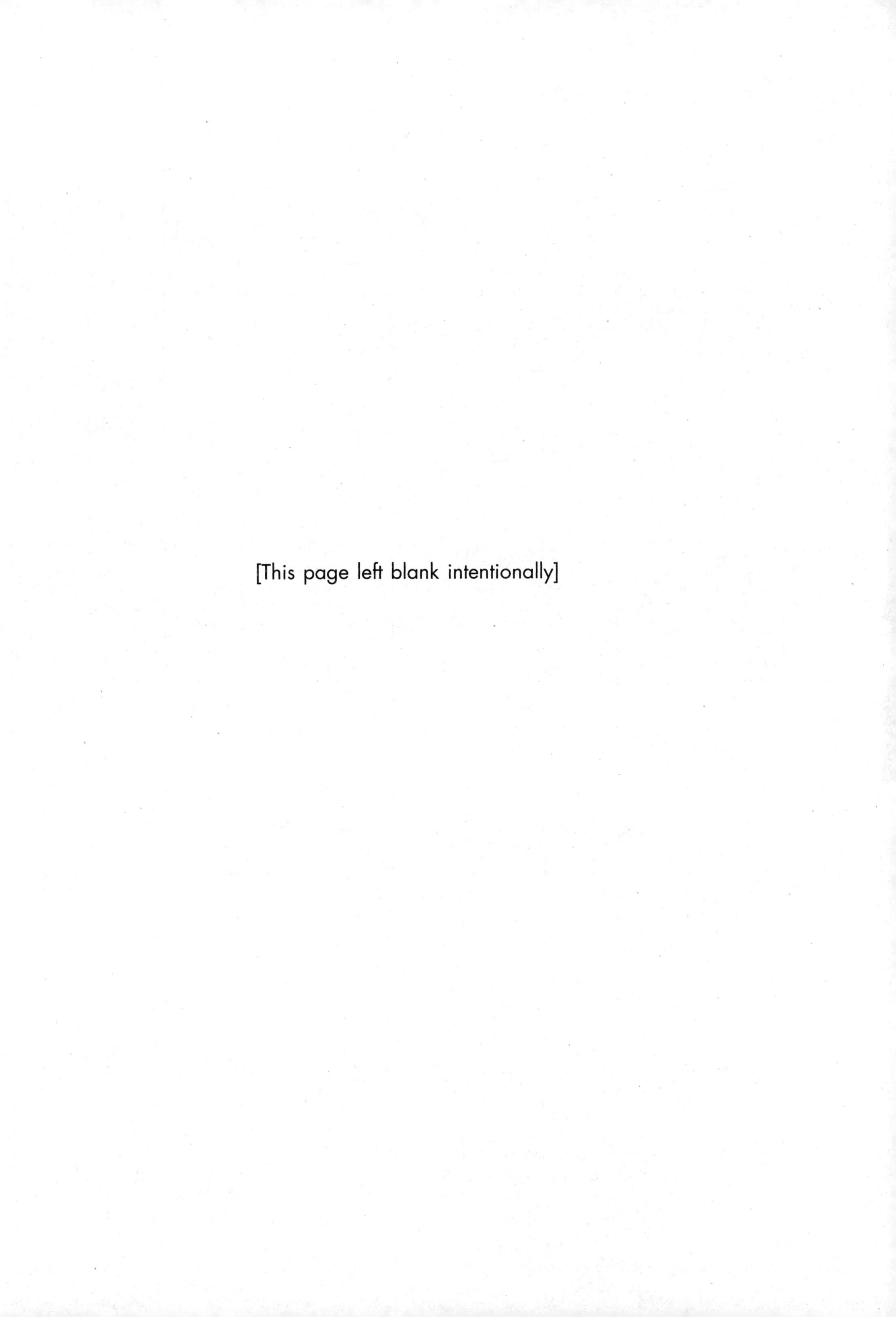
[This page left blank intentionally]

Preparing financial statements and end-of-fiscal-period entries for a corporation

1.

Applewhite Corporation

Work Sheet

For Year Ended December 31, 20 – –

	ACCOUNT TITLE	TRIAL BALANCE		ADJUSTMENTS		INCOME STATEMENT		BALANCE SHEET		
		DEBIT	CREDIT	DEBIT	CREDIT	DEBIT	CREDIT	DEBIT	CREDIT	
1	Cash	2 0 1 4 00						2 0 1 4 00		1
2	Petty Cash	4 0 0 00						4 0 0 00		2
3	Notes Receivable	3 2 0 0 00						3 2 0 0 00		3
4	Interest Receivable			(a) 6 4 00				6 4 00		4
5	Accounts Receivable	100 6 7 8 00						100 6 7 8 00		5
6	Allowance for Uncoll. Accts.		2 2 8 00		(b) 3 3 2 4 00				3 5 5 2 00	6
7	Merchandise Inventory	230 6 5 4 46			(c) 1 2 4 8 00			229 4 0 6 46		7
8	Supplies	5 1 8 5 02			(d) 4 6 1 1 50			5 7 3 52		8
9	Prepaid Insurance	11 2 0 0 00			(e) 10 0 0 0 00			1 2 0 0 00		9
10	Office Equipment	23 3 1 8 58						23 3 1 8 58		10
11	Accum. Depr.—Office Equip.		6 9 6 8 00		(f) 4 8 5 0 00				11 8 1 8 00	11
12	Store Equipment	21 7 2 7 00						21 7 2 7 00		12
13	Accum. Depr.—Store Equip.		14 5 2 8 00		(g) 3 4 8 0 00				18 0 0 8 00	13
14	Notes Payable		20 0 0 0 00						20 0 0 0 00	14
15	Interest Payable				(h) 2 5 0 00				2 5 0 00	15
16	Accounts Payable		25 7 2 6 62						25 7 2 6 62	16
17	Employee Income Tax Payable		1 9 6 7 04						1 9 6 7 04	17
18	Federal Income Tax Payable				(i) 1 0 7 3 48				1 0 7 3 48	18
19	Social Security Tax Payable		1 6 9 7 05						1 6 9 7 05	19
20	Medicare Tax Payable		4 1 0 15						4 1 0 15	20
21	Sales Tax Payable		2 0 1 4 93						2 0 1 4 93	21
22	Unemploy. Tax Pay.—Fed.		3 6 48						3 6 48	22
23	Unemploy. Tax Pay.—State		2 3 4 24						2 3 4 24	23
24	Health Ins. Premiums Pay.		5 3 7 00						5 3 7 00	24
25	Dividends Payable		6 4 0 0 00						6 4 0 0 00	25
26	Capital Stock		120 0 0 0 00						120 0 0 0 00	26
27	Retained Earnings		118 9 9 0 40						118 9 9 0 40	27
28	Dividends	25 6 0 0 00						25 6 0 0 00		28

Before Federal Income Tax:

Total of Income Statement Credit column	$1,818,777.09
Total of Income Statement Debit column	$1,722,237.44
Net Income before Federal Income Tax	$ 96,539.65

22-1 RECYCLING PROBLEM (continued)

Applewhite Corporation

Work Sheet

For Year Ended December 31, 20 – –

	Account Title	Trial Balance Debit	Trial Balance Credit	Adjustments Debit	Adjustments Credit	Income Statement Debit	Income Statement Credit	Balance Sheet Debit	Balance Sheet Credit
29	Income Summary			(c) 1,248.00		1,248.00			
30	Sales		1,801,514.54				1,801,514.54		
31	Sales Discount	4,715.49				4,715.49			
32	Sales Returns and Allowances	12,389.91				12,389.91			
33	Purchases	1,198,546.46				1,198,546.46			
34	Purchases Discount		10,494.42				10,494.42		
35	Purchases Ret. and Allow.		4,947.33				4,947.33		
36	Advertising Expense	13,189.52				13,189.52			
37	Cash Short and Over	13.50				13.50			
38	Credit Card Fee Expense	6,791.46				6,791.46			
39	Depr. Exp.—Office Equip.			(f) 4,850.00		4,850.00			
40	Depr. Exp.—Store Equip.			(g) 3,480.00		3,480.00			
41	Insurance Expense			(e) 10,000.00		10,000.00			
42	Miscellaneous Expense	33,749.04				33,749.04			
43	Payroll Taxes Expense	25,747.22				25,747.22			
44	Rent Expense	36,000.00				36,000.00			
45	Repair Expense	4,923.99				4,923.99			
46	Salary Expense	337,238.69				337,238.69			
47	Supplies Expense			(d) 4,611.50		4,611.50			
48	Uncollectible Accounts Exp.			(b) 3,324.00		3,324.00			
49	Utilities Expense	16,356.50				16,356.50			
50	Gain on Plant Assets		1,238.40				1,238.40		
51	Interest Income		518.40		(a) 64.00		582.40		
52	Interest Expense	2,880.00		(h) 250.00		3,130.00			
53	Loss on Plant Assets	1,932.16				1,932.16			
54	Federal Income Tax Expense	20,000.00		(i) 1,073.48		21,073.48			
55		2,138,451.00	2,138,451.00	28,900.98	28,900.98	1,743,310.92	1,818,777.09	408,181.56	332,715.39
56	Net Inc. after Fed. Inc. Tax					75,466.17			75,466.17
57						1,818,777.09	1,818,777.09	408,181.56	408,181.56

Federal Income Tax:	Rate	Tax
First $50,000	15%	$ 7,500.00
Next $25,000	25%	$ 6,250.00
$96,539.65 – $75,000.00 = **$21,539.65**	34%	$ 7,323.48
Total Federal Income Tax		$21,073.48

2.

Applewhite Corporation

Income Statement

For Year Ended December 31, 20 – –

					% OF NET SALES
Operating Revenue:					
Sales		1801 5 1 4 54			
Less: Sales Discount	4 7 1 5 49				
Sales Returns and Allowances	12 3 8 9 91	17 1 0 5 40			
Net Sales			1784 4 0 9 14	100.0	
Cost of Merchandise Sold:					
Merchandise Inventory, Jan. 1, 20 – –		230 6 5 4 46			
Purchases	1198 5 4 6 46				
Less: Purchases Discount	10 4 9 4 42				
Purchases Ret. and Allow.	4 9 4 7 33	15 4 4 1 75			
Net Purchases		1183 1 0 4 71			
Total Cost of Mdse. Avail. for Sale		1413 7 5 9 17			
Less Mdse. Inventory, Dec. 31, 20 – –		229 4 0 6 46			
Cost of Merchandise Sold			1184 3 5 2 71	66.4	
Gross Profit on Operations			600 0 5 6 43	33.6	
Operating Expenses:					
Advertising Expense		13 1 8 9 52			
Cash Short and Over		1 3 50			
Credit Card Fee Expense		6 7 9 1 46			
Depr. Expense—Office Equipment		4 8 5 0 00			
Depr. Expense—Store Equipment		3 4 8 0 00			
Insurance Expense		10 0 0 0 00			
Miscellaneous Expense		33 7 4 9 04			
Payroll Taxes Expense		25 7 4 7 22			
Rent Expense		36 0 0 0 00			
Repair Expense		4 9 2 3 99			
Salary Expense		337 2 3 8 69			
Supplies Expense		4 6 1 1 50			
Uncollectible Accounts Expense		3 3 2 4 00			
Utilities Expense		16 3 5 6 50			
Total Operating Expenses			500 2 7 5 42	28.0	
Income from Operations			99 7 8 1 01	5.6	

22-1   RECYCLING PROBLEM (continued)

Applewhite Corporation

Income Statement (continued)

For Year Ended December 31, 20 – –

			% OF NET SALES
Other Revenue:			
Gain on Plant Assets	1 2 3 8 40		
Interest Income	5 8 2 40		
Total Other Income		1 8 2 0 80	
Other Expenses:			
Interest Expense	3 1 3 0 00		
Loss on Plant Assets	1 9 3 2 16		
Total Other Expenses		5 0 6 2 16	
Net Deduction		3 2 4 1 36	0.2
Net Income before Federal Income Tax		96 5 3 9 65	5.4
Less Federal Income Tax Expense		21 0 7 3 48	
Net Income after Federal Income Tax		75 4 6 6 17	

4.

Applewhite Corporation

Statement of Stockholders' Equity

For Year Ended December 31, 20 – –

Capital Stock:			
$10.00 per Share			
January 1, 20 – –, 10,000 Shares Issued		100 0 0 0 00	
Issued during Current Year, 2,000 Shares		20 0 0 0 00	
Balance, December 31, 20 – –, 12,000 Shares Issued			120 0 0 0 00
Retained Earnings:			
Balance, January 1, 20 – –		118 9 9 0 40	
Net Income after Federal Income Tax for 20 – –	75 4 6 6 17		
Less Dividends Declared during 20 – –	25 6 0 0 00		
Net Increase during 20 – –		49 8 6 6 17	
Balance, December 31, 20 – –			168 8 5 6 57
Total Stockholders' Equity, December 31, 20 – –			288 8 5 6 57

5.

Applewhite Corporation

Balance Sheet

December 31, 20 – –

Assets									
Current Assets:									
Cash				2 0 1 4 00				
Petty Cash				4 0 0 00				
Notes Receivable				3 2 0 0 00				
Interest Receivable				6 4 00				
Accounts Receivable	100 6 7 8 00							
Less Allowance for Uncollectible Accounts	3 5 5 2 00		97 1 2 6 00					
Merchandise Inventory			229 4 0 6 46					
Supplies			5 7 3 52					
Prepaid Insurance			1 2 0 0 00					
Total Current Assets					333 9 8 3 98			
Plant Assets:									
Office Equipment	23 3 1 8 58							
Less Accumulated Depreciation—Office Equipment	11 8 1 8 00		11 5 0 0 58					
Store Equipment	21 7 2 7 00							
Less Accumulated Depreciation—Store Equipment	18 0 0 8 00		3 7 1 9 00					
Total Plant Assets					15 2 1 9 58			
Total Assets					349 2 0 3 56			
Liabilities									
Current Liabilities:									
Notes Payable			20 0 0 0 00					
Interest Payable			2 5 0 00					
Accounts Payable			25 7 2 6 62					
Employee Income Tax Payable			1 9 6 7 04					
Federal Income Tax Payable			1 0 7 3 48					
Social Security Tax Payable			1 6 9 7 05					
Medicare Tax Payable			4 1 0 15					
Sales Tax Payable			2 0 1 4 93					
Unemployment Tax Payable—Federal			3 6 48					
Unemployment Tax Payable—State			2 3 4 24					
Health Insurance Premiums Payable			5 3 7 00					
Dividends Payable			6 4 0 0 00					
Total Liabilities					60 3 4 6 99			
Stockholders' Equity									
Capital Stock			120 0 0 0 00					
Retained Earnings			168 8 5 6 57					
Total Stockholders' Equity					288 8 5 6 57			
Total Liabilities and Stockholders' Equity					349 2 0 3 56			

22-1   RECYCLING PROBLEM (continued)

3.

Income Statement Analysis

	Acceptable %	Actual %	Positive Result		Recommended Action If Needed
			Yes	No	
Cost of merchandise sold	Not more than 68.0%	66.4%	✓		None
Gross profit on operations	Not less than 32.0%	33.6%	✓		None
Total operating expenses	Not more than 25.0%	28.0%		✓	Review and identify excessive expenses so they may be controlled.
Income from operations	Not less than 7.0%	5.6%		✓	Controlling operating expenses will increase this percentage.
Net deduction from other revenue and expenses	Not more than 0.5%	0.2%	✓		None
Net income before federal income tax	Not less than 6.5%	5.4%		✓	Controlling operating expenses will increase this percentage.

6.

Balance Sheet Analysis

	Acceptable	Actual	Positive Result		Recommended Action If Needed
			Yes	No	
Working capital	Not less than $250,000.00	$273,636.99	✓		None
Current ratio	Between 4.0 to 1 and 6.0 to 1	5.53 to 1	✓		None

7.

GENERAL JOURNAL

PAGE 15

	DATE		ACCOUNT TITLE	DOC. NO.	POST. REF.	DEBIT	CREDIT	
1			*Adjusting Entries*					1
2	Dec.	31	*Interest Receivable*			6 4 00		2
3			*Interest Income*				6 4 00	3
4		31	*Uncollectible Accounts Expense*			3 3 2 4 00		4
5			*Allowance for Uncollectible Accounts*				3 3 2 4 00	5
6		31	*Income Summary*			1 2 4 8 00		6
7			*Merchandise Inventory*				1 2 4 8 00	7
8		31	*Supplies Expense*			4 6 1 1 50		8
9			*Supplies*				4 6 1 1 50	9
10		31	*Insurance Expense*			10 0 0 0 00		10
11			*Prepaid Insurance*				10 0 0 0 00	11
12		31	*Depreciation Expense—Office Equipment*			4 8 5 0 00		12
13			*Accumulated Depreciation—Office Equipment*				4 8 5 0 00	13
14		31	*Depreciation Expense—Store Equipment*			3 4 8 0 00		14
15			*Accumulated Depreciation—Store Equipment*				3 4 8 0 00	15
16		31	*Interest Expense*			2 5 0 00		16
17			*Interest Payable*				2 5 0 00	17
18		31	*Federal Income Tax Expense*			1 0 7 3 48		18
19			*Federal Income Tax Payable*				1 0 7 3 48	19
20								20
21								21

22-1 RECYCLING PROBLEM (continued)

8.

GENERAL JOURNAL   PAGE 16

	DATE		ACCOUNT TITLE	DOC. NO.	POST. REF.	DEBIT	CREDIT	
1			*Closing Entries*					1
2	*Dec.* 20--	31	*Sales*			1801 5 1 4 54		2
3			*Purchases Discount*			10 4 9 4 42		3
4			*Purchases Returns and Allowances*			4 9 4 7 33		4
5			*Gain on Plant Assets*			1 2 3 8 40		5
6			*Interest Income*			5 8 2 40		6
7			*Income Summary*				1818 7 7 7 09	7
8		31	*Income Summary*			1742 0 6 2 92		8
9			*Sales Discount*				4 7 1 5 49	9
10			*Sales Returns and Allowances*				12 3 8 9 91	10
11			*Purchases*				1198 5 4 6 46	11
12			*Advertising Expense*				13 1 8 9 52	12
13			*Cash Short and Over*				1 3 50	13
14			*Credit Card Fee Expense*				6 7 9 1 46	14
15			*Depreciation Expense—Office Equipment*				4 8 5 0 00	15
16			*Depreciation Expense—Store Equipment*				3 4 8 0 00	16
17			*Insurance Expense*				10 0 0 0 00	17
18			*Miscellaneous Expense*				33 7 4 9 04	18
19			*Payroll Taxes Expense*				25 7 4 7 22	19
20			*Rent Expense*				36 0 0 0 00	20
21			*Repair Expense*				4 9 2 3 99	21
22			*Salary Expense*				337 2 3 8 69	22
23			*Supplies Expense*				4 6 1 1 50	23
24			*Uncollectible Accounts Expense*				3 3 2 4 00	24
25			*Utilities Expense*				16 3 5 6 50	25
26			*Interest Expense*				3 1 3 0 00	26
27			*Loss on Plant Assets*				1 9 3 2 16	27
28			*Federal Income Tax Expense*				21 0 7 3 48	28
29		31	*Income Summary*			75 4 6 6 17		29
30			*Retained Earnings*				75 4 6 6 17	30
31		31	*Retained Earnings*			25 6 0 0 00		31
32			*Dividends*				25 6 0 0 00	32
33								33

9.

GENERAL JOURNAL

PAGE 17

	DATE		ACCOUNT TITLE	DOC. NO.	POST. REF.	DEBIT	CREDIT	
1			*Reversing Entries*					1
2	20-- Jan.	1	Interest Income			6 4 00		2
3			Interest Receivable				6 4 00	3
4		1	Interest Payable			2 5 0 00		4
5			Interest Expense				2 5 0 00	5
6		1	Federal Income Tax Payable			1 0 7 3 48		6
7			Federal Income Tax Expense				1 0 7 3 48	7
8								8
9								9
10								10

23-1 RECYCLING PROBLEM, p. D-17

Recording partners' investments and withdrawals, preparing financial statements, and liquidating a partnership

1., 5.

CASH RECEIPTS JOURNAL PAGE 11

	DATE	ACCOUNT TITLE	DOC. NO.	POST. REF.	GENERAL DEBIT	GENERAL CREDIT	ACCOUNTS RECEIVABLE CREDIT	SALES CREDIT	SALES DISCOUNT DEBIT	CASH DEBIT	
1	20-- June 15	Ashwin Akabu, Capital	R128			15 0 0 0 00				15 0 0 0 00	1
2	15	Supplies	R129		5 0 0 0 00					7 0 0 0 00	2
3		Chen Wong, Capital				12 0 0 0 00					3
4	30	Loss and Gain on Realization	R130		1 0 0 00					9 0 0 00	4
5		Merchandise Inventory				1 0 0 0 00					5
6	30	Accum. Depreciation—Equipment	R131		5 0 0 0 00					3 5 0 0 00	6
7		Equipment				7 5 0 0 00					7
8		Loss and Gain on Realization				1 0 0 0 00					8
9											9
10											10
11											11
12											12
13											13
14											14
15											15
16											16
17											17
18											18
19											19
20											20
21											21
22											22
23											23
24											24
25											25

RECYCLING PROBLEM (continued)

2., 5.

CASH PAYMENTS JOURNAL PAGE 17

	DATE	ACCOUNT TITLE	CK. NO.	POST. REF.	GENERAL		ACCOUNTS PAYABLE DEBIT	PURCHASES DISCOUNT CREDIT	CASH CREDIT	
					1 DEBIT	2 CREDIT	3	4	5	
1	20-- June 30	Chen Wong, Drawing	141		1 2 0 0 00				1 2 0 0 00	1
2	30	✔	142				1 2 5 0 00		1 2 5 0 00	2
3	30	Ashwin Akabu, Capital	143		49 9 2 0 00				90 2 1 1 00	3
4	30	Chen Wong, Capital	144		40 2 9 1 00					4
5										5
6										6
7										7
8										8
9										9
10										10
11										11
12										12
13										13
14										14
15										15
16										16
17										17
18										18
19										19
20										20
21										21
22										22
23										23
24										24
25										25

23-1   RECYCLING PROBLEM (continued)

2., 5.

GENERAL JOURNAL PAGE 21

	DATE		ACCOUNT TITLE	DOC. NO.	POST. REF.	DEBIT	CREDIT	
1	June 30		Ashwin Akabu, Drawing	M74		9 0 0 00		1
2			Purchases				9 0 0 00	2
3		30	Loss and Gain on Realization	M75		9 0 0 00		3
4			Ashwin Akabu, Capital				4 5 0 00	4
5			Chen Wong, Capital				4 5 0 00	5
6								6
7								7
8								8
9								9
10								10
11								11
12								12
13								13
14								14
15								15
16								16
17								17
18								18
19								19
20								20
21								21
22								22
23								23
24								24
25								25
26								26
27								27
28								28
29								29
30								30
31								31
32								32
33								33

3.

Total Toys

Distribution of Net Income Statement

For Month Ended June 30, 20 – –

Ashwin Akabu		
50.0% of Net Income	3 6 0 0	00
Chen Wong		
50.0% of Net Income	3 6 0 0	00
Net Income	7 2 0 0	00

23-1 RECYCLING PROBLEM (concluded)

4.

Total Toys

Owners' Equity Statement

For Month Ended June 30, 20 – –

Ashwin Akabu			
Capital, June 1, 20 – –	31 7 7 0 00		
Plus Additional Investment	15 0 0 0 00		
Total		46 7 7 0 00	
Share of Net Income	3 6 0 0 00		
Less Withdrawals	9 0 0 00		
Net Increase in Capital		2 7 0 0 00	
Capital, June 30, 20 – –			49 4 7 0 00
Chen Wong			
Capital, June 1, 20 – –	25 4 4 1 00		
Plus Additional Investment	12 0 0 0 00		
Total		37 4 4 1 00	
Share of Net Income	3 6 0 0 00		
Less Withdrawals	1 2 0 0 00		
Net Increase in Capital		2 4 0 0 00	
Capital, June 30, 20 – –			39 8 4 1 00
Total Owners' Equity, June 30, 20 – –			89 3 1 1 00

24-1 RECYCLING PROBLEM, p. D-18

Recording international and Internet sales

1., 2.

CASH RECEIPTS JOURNAL

PAGE 23

	DATE		ACCOUNT TITLE	DOC. NO.	POST. REF.	GENERAL DEBIT	GENERAL CREDIT	ACCOUNTS RECEIVABLE CREDIT	SALES CREDIT	SALES DISCOUNT DEBIT	CASH DEBIT	
						1	2	3	4	5	6	
1	20-- Nov.	7	✔	TS330	✔				8 4 5 0 00		8 4 5 0 00	1
2		12	✔	M65	✔				11 8 0 0 00		11 8 0 0 00	2
3		14	✔	TS331	✔				5 6 7 0 00		5 6 7 0 00	3
4		15	Time Drafts Receivable	R103			3 0 0 0 00				3 0 0 0 00	4
5		18	Time Drafts Receivable	R110			5 9 0 0 00				5 9 0 0 00	5
6		21	✔	TS332	✔				16 4 0 0 00		16 4 0 0 00	6
7		24	✔	M76	✔				7 5 0 0 00		7 5 0 0 00	7
8		28	✔	TS333	✔				3 3 0 0 00		3 3 0 0 00	8
9		30	Totals				8 9 0 0 00		53 1 2 0 00		62 0 2 0 00	9
10												10
11												11
12												12
13												13
14												14
15												15
16												16
17												17
18												18
19												19
20												20
21												21
22												22
23												23
24												24
25												25

1.

GENERAL JOURNAL

PAGE 23

	DATE		ACCOUNT TITLE	DOC. NO.	POST. REF.	DEBIT	CREDIT	
1	20-- Nov.	4	*Time Drafts Receivable*	TD72		2 2 0 0 00		1
2			*Sales*				2 2 0 0 00	2
3		30	*Time Drafts Receivable*	TD73		16 0 4 0 00		3
4			*Sales*				16 0 4 0 00	4
5								5
6								6
7								7
8								8
9								9
10								10
11								11
12								12
13								13
14								14
15								15
16								16
17								17
18								18
19								19
20								20
21								21
22								22
23								23
24								24
25								25
26								26
27								27
28								28
29								29
30								30
31								31
32								32
33								33

Extra form

Extra form

		% OF SALES

Extra form

JOURNAL

PAGE

DATE	ACCOUNT TITLE	DOC. NO.	POST. REF.	GENERAL		SALES CREDIT	CASH	
				DEBIT	CREDIT		DEBIT	CREDIT
1								
2								
3								
4								
5								
6								
7								
8								
9								
10								
11								
12								
13								
14								
15								
16								
17								
18								
19								
20								
21								
22								
23								
24								
25								

Name _______________________ Date _____________ Class _____________

Extra form

Extra form

GENERAL JOURNAL

PAGE

	DATE	ACCOUNT TITLE	DOC. NO.	POST. REF.	DEBIT	CREDIT	
1							1
2							2
3							3
4							4
5							5
6							6
7							7
8							8
9							9
10							10
11							11
12							12
13							13
14							14
15							15
16							16
17							17
18							18
19							19
20							20
21							21
22							22
23							23
24							24
25							25
26							26
27							27
28							28
29							29
30							30
31							31
32							32
33							33

Extra form

GENERAL JOURNAL   PAGE

	DATE	ACCOUNT TITLE	DOC. NO.	POST. REF.	DEBIT	CREDIT	
1							1
2							2
3							3
4							4
5							5
6							6
7							7
8							8
9							9
10							10
11							11
12							12
13							13
14							14
15							15
16							16
17							17
18							18
19							19
20							20
21							21
22							22
23							23
24							24
25							25
26							26
27							27
28							28
29							29
30							30
31							31
32							32
33							33

GENERAL LEDGER

ACCOUNT   ACCOUNT NO.

DATE	ITEM	POST. REF.	DEBIT	CREDIT	BALANCE	
					DEBIT	CREDIT

ACCOUNT   ACCOUNT NO.

DATE	ITEM	POST. REF.	DEBIT	CREDIT	BALANCE	
					DEBIT	CREDIT

ACCOUNT   ACCOUNT NO.

DATE	ITEM	POST. REF.	DEBIT	CREDIT	BALANCE	
					DEBIT	CREDIT

ACCOUNT   ACCOUNT NO.

DATE	ITEM	POST. REF.	DEBIT	CREDIT	BALANCE	
					DEBIT	CREDIT

Extra forms   **ACCOUNTS PAYABLE LEDGER**

VENDOR   VENDOR NO.

DATE	ITEM	POST. REF.	DEBIT	CREDIT	CREDIT BALANCE

VENDOR   VENDOR NO.

DATE	ITEM	POST. REF.	DEBIT	CREDIT	CREDIT BALANCE

VENDOR   VENDOR NO.

DATE	ITEM	POST. REF.	DEBIT	CREDIT	CREDIT BALANCE

VENDOR   VENDOR NO.

DATE	ITEM	POST. REF.	DEBIT	CREDIT	CREDIT BALANCE

ACCOUNTS RECEIVABLE LEDGERS

CUSTOMER   CUSTOMER NO.

DATE	ITEM	POST. REF.	DEBIT	CREDIT	DEBIT BALANCE

CUSTOMER   CUSTOMER NO.

DATE	ITEM	POST. REF.	DEBIT	CREDIT	DEBIT BALANCE

CUSTOMER   CUSTOMER NO.

DATE	ITEM	POST. REF.	DEBIT	CREDIT	DEBIT BALANCE

CUSTOMER   CUSTOMER NO.

DATE	ITEM	POST. REF.	DEBIT	CREDIT	DEBIT BALANCE